CHARM

Charm

How Magnetic Personalities Shape Global Politics

Julia Sonnevend

PRINCETON UNIVERSITY PRESS

PRINCETON AND OXFORD

Published by Princeton University Press
41 William Street, Princeton, New Jersey 08540
99 Banbury Road, Oxford OX2 6JX

press.princeton.edu

All Rights Reserved

ISBN 9780691230337
ISBN (e-book) 9780691230344

British Library Cataloging-in-Publication Data is available

Editorial: Meagan Levinson, Rachael Levay, and Erik Beranek
Production Editorial: Theresa Liu
Jacket / Cover Design: Katie Osborne
Production: Erin Suydam
Publicity: Maria Whelan and Kathryn Stevens

This book has been composed in Adobe Text and Gotham

Printed in the United States of America

10 9 8 7 6 5 4 3 2 1

CONTENTS

Introduction

Ukrainian president Volodymyr Zelensky was not a global celebrity before Russia's invasion of Ukraine in February 2022. Yet, as the invasion began, within days President Zelensky had swiftly captured many hearts worldwide. Through a powerful charm offensive on social media, he reached faraway audiences and delivered tangible results. His charm was neither superficial nor ephemeral nor incidental; it secured actual weapons for Ukraine. No other example shows better that charm is a defining feature of contemporary global politics.

When people discuss international diplomacy, they tend to characterize it in rational terms. They assume it is guided by "realpolitik," where national self-interest, narrowly conceived, determines decisions. Politics in this understanding is pragmatic and solely focused on tangible objectives. But nonrational factors enter human affairs and decision making in every corner of social interaction. Human social activities may be about money, power, or ego—but they often operate by a smile, a gesture, a hint of affection that shapes decisions, attitudes, and preferences. Politics is not immune to this basic feature of human experience. The power of charm as it shapes contemporary global politics is the topic of this book.

I look at politics as a site of performance, where politicians present heroes and villains on a stage to audiences who clap or boo in response.[1] In theater and in politics, individuals appear more important than complex processes. Political scientists have indeed described the past thirty years as a peak time in political personalization: we pay increasing attention to individual politicians and their close associates at the expense of institutions and organizations.[2] We have a declining loyalty toward parties, believing that individuals are more to be trusted. And on a variety of media platforms we are bombarded by instantaneous visual and textual representations of individual politicians, making us feel like we "know" them. Under these conditions, the personal magnetism of leaders becomes a defining feature of political power.

A form of personal magnetism often mentioned in the political context is charisma. Charisma, originating in the ancient Greek term for "divine gift," had been strongly attached to the church since Paul's letters to the early Christian community. More than one hundred years ago German sociologist Max Weber borrowed the term from its religious context and extended it into the secular realm. Weber argued that charisma is "a certain quality of an individual personality, by virtue of which he is set apart from ordinary men and treated as endowed with supernatural, superhuman, or at least specifically exceptional powers or qualities."[3] While the beginning of the definition clearly has religious origins, the second part allows a broader application in public life.

Weber also believed, in quite a modern way, that nobody is inherently charismatic. Audiences decide who possesses charismatic authority.

But Weber considered the perceptions of charisma in a world that had not yet seen the rise of Adolf Hitler, where mass media meant print newspapers, and when moving images of foreign leaders were confined to newsreels. We live in a radically different political and media environment. Professional political campaigns are now performed on a variety of media platforms for an international audience, and our everyday interactions, even with our close family, are represented and shared in a cascade of visual representations. We have the chance to interact with politicians online as if they were "just like us."

Contemporary leaders often appeal to our desire to see them as ordinary and authentic. Some win on the platform of being the person we would like to have a beer with. Their success is often tied to not the divine and supernatural quality of charisma, but something more relatable, more "everyday." This everyday magic spell politicians cast is what I call "charm." Charm is personal magnetism that rests on *proximity* to political "tribes" and manifests primarily through visual and textual communication on a variety of media platforms. To succeed in the current media environment, political leaders must appear as accessible, authentic, and relatable in their quest for power. Charm can also manifest in direct personal communication at parades, demonstrations, and political rallies.

This is distinctly different from how charisma has been traditionally understood. Charisma relies on *distance* to political citizens and is mostly expressed through exceptional rhetorical performances in a limited set of media.

Charles de Gaulle has been widely regarded as one of the most—if not the most—charismatic French leaders in history. He firmly believed that a charismatic leader should *not* appear as ordinary: he had to be somewhat withdrawn to create a certain aura of mystique or surprise around him. The ideal leader had to be grand, or even pompous.[4] De Gaulle's speeches reflected this view and centered on major concepts, lacking contemporary elements of relatability. The ten most frequently used terms in his speeches were (in this order): *France, the country, the Republic, the state, the world, the people, the nation, prosperity, peace,* and *future.*[5]

In contrast to de Gaulle's traditional, distance-based charisma, contemporary leaders must appeal to the ordinary even if they are sometimes admired as gods unconditionally. They aim to become "one" with their "tribe." Even if a politician is an American multimillionaire who owns Trump Tower in the heart of New York City, he must rally voters with messages they can identify with. Even if the politician's actual lifestyle could not be more different from that of his voters, he must perform as a person "just like you," for instance, by wearing a red "Make America Great Again" hat. Is this requirement for politicians to appear as our next-door neighbor absurd? It is. Yet this is the test they have to pass now. If politicians succeed and their performance fuses with their audience, we will identify with them, and this identification will trump other considerations. The followers will stay with the magnetic character through the ups and downs of political life, without checks and balances, cheering on as soccer fans would do for their favorite players.

Charm is two-faced: it embodies both the positive features of seduction and the negative features of deception. Charm comes from the Latin "carmen" (song, verse, incantation);

even in its etymology it refers to mediation and to the power to seduce, and sometimes mislead, through sound, text, and appearance. In politics and in everyday life, seduction and deception walk hand in hand, highlighting two sides of the same coin. There is a constant tension around charming interactions, as people are drawn to the seductive magic of charm, but at the same time express deep suspicion of it, fearing deception or charm's proximity to the uncontrollability of magic.

In early twenty-first-century politics, charm is constructed and presented in mass media and social media. Offline charm translates to mediated charm, and there are forms of charm that are specific to particular media environments. Those of us who live digital lives often move from offline presentation of charm to online and back. We talk to our family in the morning over breakfast, then post to social media, then meet somebody at the office or strike up a conversation with a stranger at a bus stop, then participate in an online meeting, then take a nap, followed by watching a presidential debate or the latest season of our favorite television show, and so on. Our presence and personality are continuously constructed in a variety of settings and on a series of media platforms. Politicians operate in a similar way, with the exception that almost all their presented personas appear in mediated contexts. Most of us never meet the "real" politician, only the politician's constructions in and by the media. Any understanding of political charm must take the "media" into consideration as a core ingredient. Social media are by no means the whole of how political leaders or would-be political leaders communicate, but they have become indispensable and form the main focus of my book.

The old charisma of the distanced and elevated leader has not completely disappeared. Even today, politicians sometimes appear larger than life, striving to be twenty-first-century messiahs,[6] and some followers behave more like worshipers than voters. As politicians present their identities to people on a number of platforms, they deploy their personal magnetism in various forms to fuse with targeted audiences.[7] They mix tools of charisma and charm to reach their goals as both charisma and charm rely on personality as a justification for authority. In some ways, contemporary politicians strive toward the role of superheroes, mixing ordinary and extraordinary qualities.

Outline of the Book

I begin by exploring the building blocks of charm. The heart of the first chapter is a new understanding of "charming interactions." Charm is everywhere—at day-care drop-offs, in factories and cafés, universities and grocery shops. But here I focus on how charm shapes national and international politics worldwide. I will discuss five techniques politicians often use to charm their audiences in the media: (1) performing authenticity—when politicians adjust their performances to appear "real" and relatable to audiences; (2) demasking—when politicians attempt to remove their official "masks" displaying either vulnerability or strength; (3) breaking from routine—the interruption of the flow of time to create minor, substitute "pseudo-events" for the media; (4) restaging—creating a controlled environment and space, an ideal stage where charm can particularly shine through; and (5) equalizing—when politicians present diverse audiences as a coherent community. While not all charming interactions of politicians include all these techniques, they are often present in moments of mediatized political charm.

I will then discuss five politicians as they present themselves in contemporary media. These politicians range from liberal to illiberal to authoritarian. Most of them use charm as a tool and occasionally as a weapon. The first is Jacinda Ardern, the youngest-ever elected prime minister of New Zealand and a famous "anti-Trump" female icon on the global stage. By the time of the publication of this book she had left politics, but not without leaving a lasting mark. Her Facebook activity presented vulnerability and mistakes as features rather than as bugs in politics. She argued for "kindness" as a keyword of twenty-first-century public life. Her leadership raised key questions around gender and political charm. She quickly became a global celebrity, an icon of the politics of kindness and the challenges of juggling motherhood and work as a millennial professional. "Jacindamania" as a term appeared in almost all articles about her as Ardern triggered admiration, but also intense rejection, likely leading to her early burnout.

A radically different leader is the lead actor of the next chapter: Viktor Orbán. In 2022 he was elected for a fourth consecutive term as Hungary's prime minister. Orbán describes himself as illiberal and presents a populist masculine charm but frequently also shares relatable moments on Facebook, such as images of himself diapering his grandchild. But most importantly, Orbán presents himself as the symbolic condensation of "Hungarian-ness," the embodiment of the nation on social media. While tasting Hungarian pastries or participating in folk rituals, he draws the boundaries of the nation and personally radiates a message of tradition, Christianity, ethnic homogeneity, and "Hungary first."

Orbán's case highlights that no political side has exclusive ownership over the power of charm. Personal magnetism will be weaponized by leaders from all corners of global political life in their quest for power.

The next two chapters will discuss so-called charm offensives. I define "charm offensive" as a strategic public relations campaign that weaponizes the personal magnetism of political leaders, selected negotiators, or other representatives to radically shift a country's international image.[8] First, we hear about Iran's attempt to alter its image as it negotiated a crucial deal with the United States on nuclear arms control in 2015. In front of Western cameras, Iran's foreign minister Mohammad Javad Zarif smiled, took intimate walks with the US secretary of state, and listened carefully to experts. His gentle and relatable behavior throughout the negotiations created an environment in which previous clashes between the two countries could be momentarily forgotten. The next chapter analyzes North Korean leader Kim Jong-un as he weaponized charm to temporarily shift North Korea's unsavory image in the West during the 2018 Korean Winter Olympics. From viral selfies to live-covered North-South meetings to even crossing the border hand in hand with the South Korean president, Kim created mesmerizing moments for Western journalists and temporarily shifted the tone of North Korean coverage. In these two chapters I focus on how charm offensives are perceived by international media.

And finally, I end with a countercase, former German chancellor Angela Merkel. Merkel achieved authenticity with her audiences, while avoiding contemporary methods of political personalization. By showing a repetitive and predictable image on social media, she did not adhere to media platforms' inclination for drama and spectacle. Merkel still managed to establish a strong and often admired political image on the global stage. She showed that it is possible to succeed without the weaponization of charm. But her case might be unique given Germany's exceptionally negative historical experiences with charisma in the twentieth century, leading to widespread distrust of charismatic political performances among German voting publics.

All these politicians show important aspects of how to use and how not to use charm in current public life to manufacture authenticity. Despite their differences, they often play with, or in Merkel's case almost ostentatiously play against, techniques to seduce their audiences. Depending on your political views you might perceive these attempts to charm as alluring seduction or destructive deception. Yet, it is hard to deny their political power.

Charm will shape the future of democracy worldwide, as political values and ideals will be increasingly embodied by people and personalities, presented to political tribes in a wide variety of media. As new actors enter the world stage, we will experience moments of hope when charm will support what we perceive as valuable causes, but also crushing times of despair when charm will become a tool for destruction. Charm will be a key method of twenty-first-century diplomacy, weaponized in the forms of charm offensives around the world in a wide variety of political systems from democratic to illiberal to authoritarian (and all the gray zones in between). Charm will always be two-faced, oscillating between seduction and deception, subject to individual and group evaluation. While I could easily paint either a dark or a rosy picture about charm's impact on global politics, the reality is more complex. Both seduction and deception will be present. Charm will make a difference in human affairs and public life, especially in an era of direct and reciprocal verbal and visual communications between leaders and their audiences. Charm will also be a crucial element in the constitution of political leadership and political authenticity. This book is an attempt to give political charm its due, to portray its varieties on the international stage, and to suggest that this bit of political magic should be—and can be—better understood.

1

Charm

A KEYWORD OF CONTEMPORARY GLOBAL POLITICS

A charming person draws you in like a vacuum cleaner. You may or may not want to resist—but you are going along. It is a bit like a dance, a gentle push and pull, where you figure out the steps and often just go with the flow. The magic occurs between you and the charming person, in a particular place and time. It matters if you meet in a museum or at the local bodega. It matters how much time you have, what the weather is like, and how you feel that day. If everything aligns, you connect to the other person's performance and lose your focus, critical stance, and somewhat even your consciousness. If it does not work, you regard the performance as fake—you may even feel cheated.

Charm is the ability to attract or delight as if by magic. The charming person casts a "magic spell" and makes you feel good about yourself. Magic, by definition, is magical because it is undefinable. If you try to capture a butterfly, you are killing it just by your attempt to analyze. Social scientists are particularly good at this destructive behavior—we aim to catch, and by thorough analysis, paralyze living things. We call this behavior "constructing clear definitions," but the outcome is a jargoned, lifeless writing no human being, except perhaps the author, would find enjoyable.

The challenges of defining cannot stop us from trying to understand elusive things that frequently shift their shapes. There are several other terms we have never been fully able to define, and yet they change our lives in major ways. It has proven to be rather difficult to define *humor*. Be prepared to read the most boring definitions of your life! One of the most influential definitions managed to say almost nothing about humor: "We define a humor-soliciting stimulus as any social and non-social event, occurring purposely or inadvertently, that is perceived to be amusing."[1] What would not fit under this definition?

Luck is another term that is central to life yet quite hard to capture with words.[2] Until very recently, sociology has been almost completely silent about luck, basically ignoring both the concept and its influence on social life. Yet, who could describe one's life trajectory without mentioning luck? Whose future will not involve a moment of unpredictable magic?

Social work professor and mental-health guru Brené Brown thrives on defining undefinable qualities. She particularly takes pride in her atypical definition of "love":

> We cultivate love when we allow our most vulnerable and powerful selves to be deeply seen and known, and when we honor the spiritual connection that grows from that offering with trust, respect, kindness and affection.[3]

It is possible to attack this definition from all sorts of directions. Brown knows this but prefers to have a vulnerable definition over having none.

In all these cases, crucial aspects of social life have been discarded or simply ignored by researchers, because they were hard to capture. Scientists struggled to define them, so they opted to look the other way. I believe the same has happened to personal magnetism and its various manifestations from charisma to charm.

The foundational theory of charisma by German sociologist Max Weber from the early twentieth century was vague.[4] Weber recognized that charisma is measured and decided by the performer's audience and that the person perceived as charismatic had to accept and act on this designation. Charisma thus emerged in an interpersonal relationship between the followers and the person they perceived as charismatic. Weber also noted charisma's revolutionary force, its promise to bring change, and its inherent instability, as charisma falters if the leader is not able to bring the proposed reform. These observations are still relevant today as we try to identify the power of personal magnetism. But Weber failed to ever define what charisma ultimately contained. This bug was a feature in some ways, as it emphasized charisma's magic and its shifting shape in distinct contexts.

The ability to capture hearts with personal magnetism is central to success in business, everyday conversations, and even politics today. Yet, paradoxically, we often present a rational understanding of social and public life, one built on the careful weighing of facts and calm deliberation. But nonrationality is everywhere in social interactions. Whether or not we are afraid of taming charm because it is unknowable and incomprehensible, charm shapes our social interactions from birth to death. As one journalist put it during the 2008 presidential elections in the United States: "Obama offers that 'something'—call it charm, charisma, a positive vision for the future, a voice of empowerment, a role model for youth— Obama has 'it.'"[5] Understanding that special "it" as it shapes political power is the task.

Why write a book about a term we cannot ultimately define? I will certainly not propose a straitjacket definition of charm that works in every context. That is a limitation I must accept at the beginning. But I can still dissect charm's most common manifestations in politics and analyze its repeated techniques in the media. My aim is to try to get as close to contemporary mediated political charm as possible.

The Charming Interaction

The first step is to think through the Lego blocks of charming interactions. Charm is a performance, put on display. It begins with stimulation when people entering a social interaction express themselves to others. Audiences then perceive and evaluate this stimulation. The charming interaction happens in a particular space, the "stage," even when it is not mediated. The physical, material circumstances of the interaction will also shape its perception. In an ideal case, the performer (the charmer) on the stage fuses with the audience: in some ways they become as one.[6] If the performance is successful, audiences find it authentic, relatable, and seductive. In these exceptional moments, audiences experience a dramatic breakthrough of personality. When the performance is not successful, people perceive it as fake, disconnected, or deceptive. Ultimately, the audience decides whether a performance is charming, and when it decides, it mobilizes values, beliefs, and cultural upbringings.[7]

Temporal factors also influence the charming interaction, particularly in the quickly shifting cultures of contemporary media. A performance that is deemed as "authentically charming" in a given moment may fall into the category of "cringe" only a little time later. In these cases the performance breaks down and ultimately fails. The reverse is also true: cringe can turn into charming, if the conditions change and the audiences' evaluation shift, turning a failed performance into a successful one.

Throughout the charming interaction, the "charmer" will try to capture your heart, making you feel like the only person who matters. Have you ever read a news profile of President Bill Clinton that does not mention his ability to make you feel exceptionally important? According to many accounts, he magically "worked the room," making everyone feel they were heard and seen. For some, his charm became lethal, as it was put by former White House intern Monica Lewinsky, with whom Clinton had a brief affair: "I was enamored with him, like many others, he had a charisma to him—and it was a lethal charm, and I was intoxicated."[8]

Yet, beyond the general ability to "single you out," it is challenging to capture the actual tools of charm. But there is now an extensive industry built on the belief that the components of charm can be identified and even taught. They offer workshops and books to quickly teach you this "skill" for an exorbitant fee (I admit I am sometimes tempted to join this industry, when academia seems unbearably confining). Researchers have extensively studied the various methods charmers as performers use to achieve fusion with their audiences. These methods include looking into your eyes, nodding, a careful but powerful selection of metaphors, expressive language, eloquence, presentation of appealing vision, deep voice, speaking slowly, and having a mindful presence, among others.[9] The list of methods is long, and often contradictory. While some authors want you to nod more, others expect less nodding. Whether learned or just accidentally acquired, using these methods, the charmer aims to make you feel as the one and only in the world: seen, respected, and loved.

In contemporary mass societies the enchantment of being the "one and only in the world" is real. When many feel they are simply statistics and just part of the crowd, the ability to single out a person as an individual has a powerful appeal. Charm offers the person being charmed the chance to stand out and to be recognized as a valuable human being. In the moment of recognition, we shine the brightest as a unique and appreciated member of society. When the charmers perform their magic with the help of social media, television, radio, or other forms of media, we are looking for this feeling of recognition, understanding and connection.

As British media scholar Paddy Scannell put it, the media address the masses individually, recognizing "anyone as someone."[10] Politicians harness this power of mass media to generate charm. The media construct, represent, and narrate charm to us in a bundle of images and texts. But even narration does not really capture the relationship. On social media, people often brand themselves as charming and authentic, leaving other narrators out of the picture.[11] It is no longer about the media simply representing charm, as our media images are inherent to our self-image, making it increasingly hard to even separate the "real" from the "mediated."

Throughout history, human beings have presented their personal magnetism to others, in one form or another. But until the widespread adoption of online visual media, we have not frequently moved our personality to mediated environments. Newspapers occasionally represented people, and over time radio and television showed voices and images of celebrities and everyday people.[12] But it is a relatively recent situation that we, ordinary people, on an hourly basis, present our faces, voices, and interaction on screen. How personal magnetism is constructed and imagined is defined by this strange "transport" from offline to online and back.

It is challenging enough to charm in everyday life too, but the challenges are truly daunting on media platforms. How can we translate personal magnetism, a distinctive quality of individuals, to media spheres, where the personal touch can easily get lost? What changes? You are dealing with a diverse and fragmented audience. The performer acts on a virtual stage. Even basic features of the charming interaction, such as looking into the eyes of your conversation partner, are all but impossible.

When it comes to public life, we meet politicians almost exclusively in mediated spaces—except for those occasional, well-planned handshakes and speeches at election events.[13] Politicians must cast that magic spell in mediated spaces: charming politicians must perform on mediated stages. Their personalities become ever more important to shape the image of their countries domestically and internationally. When people have a negative view of a country's political leader, this will influence their judgment of the country itself.[14] The perception of a foreign country's leader shapes people's decisions about whether to support sending military aid, whether to buy products from the country, or even whether to visit it as tourists.[15] Countries' leaders and their close associates thus serve as cognitive shortcuts or source cues to navigate complex and confusing information landscapes.

Contemporary politicians effectively work as influencers, embracing the "influencer industrial ethos," as communication scholar Emily Hund called it.[16] They provide consistent and relatable content on social media and then leverage the rewards, although often in less direct economic terms than regular influencers use. Still, their mind-set is the same: they generate loyal communities by producing consistent online content for their "tribe" and for those who attack their tribe. The audience's appreciation is thoroughly measured, quantified, packaged, and sold.

Often politicians' visual appearance, their very own bodies, come to represent a complex set of ideologies.[17] This connection between the perception of a leader and his or her country is of course absurd if we think only in rational terms. While President Trump brought a political stance radically different from President Obama's, the country did not change radically in January 2017. There were elements of "Trumpism" beforehand, and elements of "Obamaism" stayed on. Yet, international audiences perceived the country fundamentally differently.

Whether politicians can fuse with their audiences nationally and internationally is increasingly important yet ever more complicated. How can politicians ever recreate the everyday magic of charming interaction in fragmented, global, and online spaces? How can they fuse with their audiences? The methods depend on the performer, the audience, the setting. The best would be to say: "all this is context specific." But after reviewing the literature of charisma and

TABLE 1.1. Five Techniques Employed during the Charming
Interaction

1. Performing authenticity

Adjusting the performance to appear "real" and relatable to audiences

2. Demasking

Attempting to remove the performer's mask, displaying either
vulnerability or strength

3. Breaking from routine

Interrupting the flow of time to create minor, substitute
"pseudo-events"

4. Restaging

Creating a controlled environment and space, an ideal stage where
charm can particularly shine through

5. Equalizing

Presenting diverse audiences as a coherent community

charm in a variety of academic disciplines and doing years of
empirical research on charm in many national contexts, I was
able to identify some recurring strategies politicians (and
others) use to connect through the media with fragmented,
international audiences. Not all politicians use all these techniques, but many deploy a combination of them in addition
to some unique, individual characteristics (table 1.1).

PERFORMING AUTHENTICITY

We all know that the media manufacture reality, yet we paradoxically look for authentic performances on our screens.[18]
Charm and the quest for authenticity are closely related. At
the heart of charm is the ability to project authenticity, to

appear real, relatable, and spontaneous. If the charmer fails to appear as genuinely charming, his or her performance will be deemed "fake." The audience may still acknowledge the attempt to charm but will see it as manufactured. The irony of the quest for authenticity is that contemporary political campaigns are anything but authentic; they are put together by a dismaying number of speech writers, personal secretaries, spinners, poll takers, and focus groups, along with donor input and the like.[19] The candidates still visit diners and local factories, but most of their constituencies meet them through screens. While candidates are almost fully detached from ordinary human reality, with a meticulously planned schedule that barely allows bathroom visits, they are expected to appear as authentic—as one of us.

This appearance of being like us has almost nothing to do with politicians' ability to succeed in the jobs they seek. As communication scholar Zizi Papacharissi put it, "we forget to realize that it is not humanly possible for someone to be a capable leader of a country and act like our next-door neighbor. There is a reason why our next-door neighbor is not running for office, after all."[20] Being good at petting dogs or playing with children is not what politicians need to perform well in high-level bureaucracy. Yet, paradoxically, this is what we expect from our leaders.

Let's consider a few examples of this paradox of demanding authenticity in political performances. In May 2009, a "scandal" rocked the Obama presidency. In a popular diner in Virginia, President Obama ordered a cheeseburger with Vice President Joe Biden. But he asked for a special condiment: Dijon mustard. Conservative political commentators quickly capitalized on this moment, presenting him as a member of a faraway elite. Right-wing TV host Sean Hannity joked, "Plain old ketchup, well it didn't quite cut it for the president," and he labeled Obama's order a "fancy burger."[21] Former secretary of state Hillary Clinton walked into similar traps during her presidential campaign in 2016. On a visit to New York City, she struggled five times to swipe her MetroCard at the subway station—a moment that quickly became a symbol of her detached elitism.[22] In another case, she visited an East Harlem apartment, and cameras captured her apparent shock at the living conditions, quickly prompting related jokes and memes.[23] In all these cases, politicians appeared to some audiences as "out of place," disconnected from the working class and mainstream America, and deeply inauthentic. Yet, ordering a "fancy burger" or struggling with a MetroCard has very little to do with what it takes to be a successful American president.

This incessant search for an authentic politician is coupled with a strong sense of inauthenticity in politics.[24] Politicians are continuously subject to our authenticity tests, in terms of both their leadership abilities and their personal lives.[25] Our authenticity tests require authenticity not only in action, but also in looks. During the campaigning for the 2024 US Republican presidential nomination, Florida governor Ron DeSantis was frequently accused of wearing cowboy boots with height-boosting insoles so that he could successfully compete with taller candidates. Posts mocking the governor were viewed by millions on social media, triggering an intense debate, even involving expert shoemakers.[26] Again, authentic looks have little to do with political expertise, yet voters increasingly demand authenticity performances in every aspect of political candidates' lives. While running our frequent tests on politicians, we expect authenticity removed from the actual requirements and contexts of professional politics. Paradoxically, we look for a performance of authenticity that radiates transparency.

Authenticity is a key performative requirement of populist politics as well. Populist politicians regularly attack establishment figures as inauthentic and vehemently claim authenticity for themselves. In their disruptive performances, populists argue that their more traditional political opponents do everything in a strategic, meticulously planned, and ultimately inauthentic form.[27] At the heart of populism is the imagination that, with the arrival of the populist politician, politics would finally become "real." Instead of disconnected urban bureaucrats, the true voice of the public enters the political sphere. As one rural Wisconsin interviewee put it to political scientist Katherine Cramer, voters have had enough of urban elites who "shower before work, not afterwards."[28] Populists continuously perform to audiences on the global stage using a distinct communication style, while pretending to be their authentic selves untouched by the rules and habits of elite politics.[29] Hiding this deep contradiction is essential for their success.

Establishment politicians struggle to defend themselves from populist attacks on their authenticity. The more time they have spent in professional politics, the less likely they can claim genuine and honest connection to everyday, ordinary life. Their main chance is to counter the populist's spectacular authenticity performance with the message of "expertise." Still, the irony of this battle is that neither the populist nor the establishment figure is "one of us." Their campaigns are strategic and planned, and we all know this but somehow block out that knowledge. Moreover, populist politicians have often spent multiple decades in elite politics (not all populists are newcomers as Donald J.

Trump is), making the "outsider" performance even more challenging.[30]

Indian prime minister Narendra Modi brought the performance of authenticity to a whole new level when he started to introduce 3D holographic speeches during his 2014 campaign. Many voters stayed after rallies to see if Narendra Modi was really there.[31] These powerful moments of the "suspension of disbelief" likely contributed to Modi's election success in 2014.[32] The future will hold many similar attempts at pretending to "be there" as a quasi next-door neighbor with the help of swiftly shifting technologies.

Politicians also use iconic objects that mark them as both extraordinary and ordinary in their quest for authenticity. A key example is the red MAGA cap that displays Trump's key slogan "Make America Great Again." The cap was a hallmark of his successful 2016 campaign and has remained omnipresent at his rallies. The cap broadly signifies belonging and resentment, yet its actual content is hard to define. Presidents Reagan (a Republican) and Clinton (a Democrat) both used the slogan before.[33] Still, the combination of a wearable object with a flexible message created a distinct identity for MAGA and an authentic appearance for Donald J. Trump.

The authenticity performance works in a larger context of "affective politics,"[34] where we increasingly *feel* our way into politics. When looking at a political performance, we mobilize a vast army of emotions from awe to resignation to hate. Our connection to the candidate is often not based on careful deliberation or a thorough filtering of facts: we look for emotional connection and the reassurance of our existing beliefs and identities.[35] The candidates strategically present authenticity to us as a value and an image to look for.[36] Authenticity must be performed effortlessly, providing the illusion that all this is "real" and "natural." Ultimately the authenticity performance, when it works, puts the politician in sync with his or her audience, triggering a strong emotional bond and the construction of a community or even a tribe. The belonging to this community then trumps other, more rational considerations.

DEMASKING

The official role of politicians often clashes with their attempts to appear as "one of us." In 2022, during Russia's invasion of Ukraine, President Biden gave a speech in Warsaw. It turned out to be one of the historic speeches of his presidency: the invasion, he said, signaled an existential fight between democracies and autocracies worldwide. At the end of the speech, he suddenly said something unexpected, even for his advisers, who had gone through multiple drafts of his talk. Biden suddenly exclaimed, "For God's sake, this man cannot remain in power" (referring to Russian president Vladimir Putin). The sentence rocked social media worldwide and scared the White House staff sufficiently to issue an immediate statement: "The President's point was that Putin cannot be allowed to exercise power over his neighbors or the region. He was not discussing Putin's power in Russia, or regime change."[37] Yet, it was a powerful moment of demasking. President Biden, who had just met Ukrainian refugees before the speech, captured the mood of refugee-packed Warsaw. He said what many were thinking, and for a moment he seemed to have forgotten the other "hat" he was wearing, that of the president of the United States, who is expected to tread carefully in diplomatic matters.

Many also remember the moment when President George W. Bush first heard the news of the 9/11 terrorist attacks. He happened to be visiting an elementary school in Sarasota to read *The Pet Goat* with children, when his chief of staff whispered into his ears that a second plane had hit the World Trade Center in the New York City. In a famous picture that captured the moment, Bush sat in front of a school sign: "reading makes a country great."[38] In his attempt to "demask," to be part of a regular school day, he was suddenly brutally reminded of his formal role as the president of the United States—and he quickly left the school to attend to his job. His plane took off before he even had the chance to sit down.

Demasking is the performer's attempt to remove his or her "official" mask and appear as an everyday human being. Demasking is a distinct form of authenticity that detaches politicians from their official roles and makes them appear as "everyday" persons. Demasking means dropping the formalities of the politicians' roles and engaging in regular interactions. Politicians often go to sports events or participate in school classes or bring flowers to retirement homes to perform everyday habitual acts. Sometimes these interactions work, and politicians gather sympathy; other times their attempts appear as fake or forced or even cringeworthy. They also often have to abruptly return to their official jobs, leaving their "next-door neighbor" image behind.

BREAKING FROM ROUTINE

During the first ever visit of an Indian prime minister to Israel in 2017, Narendra Modi walked with his Israeli counterpart Benjamin Netanyahu barefoot into water at a beach in northern Israel. The event was closed to journalists, but the Israeli government selected some images and videos for global distribution. The visually spectacular scenes of an unusual political bonding were produced for the media and received the attention intended. On Netanyahu's Twitter account a related pic was shared with the title: "there is nothing like going to the beach with friends."[39] There was as little spontaneity as friendship in this picture, but it reached the planned results.

An event creates a rupture in the repetitive flow of everyday life. As sociologist Robin Wagner-Pacifici put it, in these moments of rupture "the world seems out of whack, and everyday routines are, at least, disrupted."[40] Politicians have always designed events that could attract interest. And many events are directly staged for the media. Media scholars have very conflicting views on these events. Already in 1962, Daniel Boorstin denounced events that were manufactured for press coverage, labeling them as "pseudo-events."[41] He also warned about the rise of the celebrity, a "human pseudo event" who is "well-known for his well-knownness."[42] In contrast, thirty years later Daniel Dayan and Elihu Katz recognized "media events" as potentially cohesive for societies.[43] Dayan and Katz focused on preplanned, ceremonial events, covered live by television, for instance, the funeral of President Kennedy and the first wedding of Prince Charles, that could bring societies together in a common viewing experience. These traditional media events are still present in the current media ecology: just consider the extensive ceremonial aspect of US presidential inaugurations or the spectacle of the Olympic Games. But there are new, more ephemeral events on the rise, particularly on social media.

Sometimes events leave no choice for the politician but to react. Japanese politicians had to address the Fukushima nuclear disaster, and reluctant officials had to grapple with the aftermath of the Wenchuan earthquake in China.[44] There was no way an American president could ignore an event of the magnitude of 9/11. But smaller events that occur in the world leave some options for how, and how much, to attend to them. The media also provide politicians with abundant chances to manufacture events of public interest. Social media platforms offer sites for quickly emerging and then disappearing happenings. These minor events suck audiences in, providing us with the feeling of "eventfulness." We may even go down some "rabbit hole" on the internet to research these happenings. But as quickly social media events or scandals appear, they also fade. Building a lasting image of political authenticity on ephemeral events is rarely feasible.

RESTAGING

In November 2021, New Zealand's prime minister Jacinda Ardern uploaded a quick post to Facebook: "I was meant to do a Facebook live tonight but I left it too late so instead, here's a pic of me standing in front of a generic door at Premier House, and a written version of what I would have said!"[45] With this "trick," Ardern pretended that her audience is part of her inner team—with access to offstage images and even her speech drafts. While appearing to be spontaneous, Ardern in fact highly controlled the stage of the interaction.

In November 2021, Canadian prime minister Justin Trudeau met US vice president Kamala Harris on a balcony of the Eisenhower Executive Office Building in Washington, DC (fig. 1.1). By moving outside, where they were able

FIG. 1.1.   US vice president Kamala Harris and Canadian prime minister Justin Trudeau speak on a balcony of the Eisenhower Executive Office Building in Washington, DC, November 18, 2021. REUTERS / Kevin Lamarque.

to interact without masks during the ongoing coronavirus pandemic, the two political leaders also signaled intimacy and mutual understanding. By restaging the interaction from a regular office scene, they made a routine meeting more spectacular for the media.

Charming interactions happen at a particular site in a certain location. This site is the "stage" on which the performance is enacted. The performer sometimes manipulates the stage to achieve the ideal interaction: this is "restaging." For instance, if the performer would like to showcase the accidental, vulnerable aspect of an interaction, he or she will highlight failures of the stage—maybe the camera angle is wrong, or the site is unappealing or even shocking. By changing the stage, the performer reframes the interaction and suggests desired interpretations. In producing the ideal stage and interaction, politicians often turn to "authenticity illusions," which range from minor lighting adjustments and sound effects to more drastic postproduction editing and photoshopping.[46]

Sometimes contemporary political leaders also invite audiences to the backstage of their practices. On social media they might present their offices or introduce their staff members. By inviting audiences to the backstage, they project relatability, authenticity, and ordinariness. The stage provides viewers with context and something tangible. Stages that are familiar to us can even bring the performer closer to our hearts. Unusual, spectacular, or awkward sites also work well, capturing the audiences' attention, triggering guessing games about where the attempts to charm and fuse were performed. Restaging also often appears as "unstaging," communicating that there is no stage, there is no performance, but we are delving into the realms of the "real."

EQUALIZING

To achieve fusion with the audience, the performers must remove as many barriers as possible. While they are detached from the everyday life of their fragmented audiences, they need to present the audience as fundamentally homogenous and "one" with them. The diverse social media audience is presented as a close-knit community. Ultimately, if everything aligns, the charmers' performances fuse with their audience.

American presidents often emphasize unity in their speeches, especially after bruising campaigns. Just consider Joe Biden's inaugural speech in January 2021: "We can see each other not as adversaries but as neighbors. We can treat each other with dignity and respect. We can join forces, stop the shouting, and lower the temperature. For without unity there is no peace, only bitterness and fury. No progress, only exhausting outrage. No nation, only a state of chaos."[47] Here the unity of the audience is set as the condition for the very existence of the nation.

There's a large complication here for leaders who make their way to prominence by making some segments of the population the enemy—they address not "all the people" but only "the real people"—the true Americans or Brazilians or Mexicans who hold true to a set of traditions or values. Populist leaders often try to capture attention with the strategic division of their audience.[48] They distinguish between a homogenous and an antagonistic group, the "pure people" and the "corrupt elite."[49] They often draw further distinctions between "us" and "them." The "other" could be the LGBTQ community, the Roma, the left, the right, the liberals, communities of color, migrants, NGOs, or selected personal enemies like American financier and philanthropist George Soros. By talking to and about an imagined, ideal audience, populists draw the boundaries of their intended audiences.

The Perception of Charm, or Who Do We Trust?

Charm is a matter of evaluation: it is the audience who decides whether a performance is charming or not. A charming interaction may leave you satisfied, but you could also regret it afterward, feeling a bit tricked or ashamed. There is a saying in French, "avoir l'esprit d'escalier," for coming up with the right reaction much later, when the interaction is all over and you are already at the "bottom of the stairs."[50] The charming interaction works in a similar way. You may find your vocabulary and wit to respond, for instance in an online comment, but sometimes you see the entire exchange in a radically different light once the spell is over. Indeed, charm is a magic spell, and depending on how you judge the outcome, it might be a blessing or a curse.

Sometimes charm turns into deception in your perception once circumstances change. Consider a messy divorce. You fell in love with Prince Charming, Mr. Seduction, but after the divorce you feel that in fact you married Mr. Deception. Did the person change? Did your perception change? Perhaps both? Rupture points like divorces show how fragile these categories are. Seduction is often met with suspicion.[51] In the Judeo-Christian tradition, the seduction of Eve is associated with the loss of Paradise. In later mythologies of seduction, the seducer is engaged in serial destruction and leaves broken hearts behind. In a recent rendering of *Don Giovanni* at the Metropolitan Opera in New York, the charmer was presented as a serial abuser, a character from a contemporary #metoo scandal, whose destructive behavior darkens the world and destroys the lives of women around him.[52] Mozart's opera allows so many interpretations because of the duality in our evaluations of charming interactions: they range from seduction (in which Don Giovanni is perceived as a romantic hero) to deception (where Don Giovanni is understood as unredeemable and destructive).

There is a prevalent mind-set of distrust that still pervades our understanding and perception of charm and often leads to distancing in evaluation of charming interactions. When I mention this book's topic in casual conversations with people on planes, in grocery stores, or in my child's school, they are fascinated but often add, "I am suspicious of charming people." This deep ambivalence around charm strongly shapes charm's perception in global and national politics.

Our level of trust toward a politician is also shaped by our political identities. When faced with an election outcome that is hard to accept, researchers and regular voters often turn to the easy explanation of "disinformation": the other side must be lacking information if deciding to vote in a particular way. But a more recent explanation of these election shocks argues that our understanding of "tribes" often precedes or trumps our preferences for certain policies. As political communication scholar Dannagal Goldthwaite Young argued, "many Americans' political identities don't necessarily capture a specific slate of policy positions as much as they capture an entire way of life."[53]

In political contexts, voters may have an already-established minimum level of trust if the candidate fits the social group category they prefer. Politicians thus often communicate which social groups they find "ideal." Political communication scholars Daniel Kreiss, Regina Lawrence, and Shannon McGregor have called this "identity ownership."[54] In their view, Trump effectively communicated that he was the ultimate representation of white conservative

America, triggering identification with his image even if the voter disagreed with some of his policy suggestions. The perception of charm is thus closely linked to the question how much we trust the performer and the group he aims to represent. If there is an already-established pattern of trust, the charmer may get away with more than otherwise. On the other hand, limited trust can raise the bar for charm to shine through. Former first lady Michelle Obama powerfully describes in her memoir how careful they needed to be as the first African American family aiming for the highest office in the country. Speaking of Barack Obama's presidential campaign, she wrote, "We knew that as a black candidate he couldn't afford any sort of stumble. He'd have to do everything twice as well."[55] In this case lack of trust in some voters due to the politician's race raised the bar for the evaluation of the politician's every move.

The Dangers of Charm

Charming people delight us, elevate us, and sometimes capture our hearts. Charm can collapse walls between people and resolve delicate situations, for instance, in high-stakes diplomatic negotiations. But charm can also lead us into tunnels that we should avoid. The abuser and the fraudster often need to be charming to convince us to do something that we really should not do. Fraudsters and criminals from investment adviser Bernie Madoff to Fyre festival organizer Billy McFarland to financier Jeffrey Epstein have all been described as charming. Charm is often present in abusive relationships and toxic workplaces, and it is a characteristic linked with psychopathy. A growing literature in management studies on corporate "assholes" is also grappling with the power of charm as it shapes company culture. Stanford business professor Robert I. Sutton wrote a series of books on how to handle asshole-saturated workplaces, and his global success shows the omnipresence of this issue. In his view, we live in the era of "peak asshole," when mean-spirited behavior is worse than ever.[56] Charm's dangers are clear and present.

Not all abusers and fraudsters are charming; they have other tools too, from threat to disinformation to gaslighting to a fake presentation of expertise. But charm is often their most important power. As a broadcaster said about American former football running back O. J. Simpson, soon after the brutal murder of Simpson's wife, Simpson was a "rascal," "but, as you know, he's charming and he's in that athletic world that winks at that."[57] Charm often serves as the explanation for what cannot be justified.

The Role of Social Media Platforms

While political campaigns started to introduce blogs in 2004, the first real social media campaign in the United States was Barack Obama's in 2008.[58] Ever since, social media platforms have become increasingly present in political campaigns. Currently, more people receive news from Facebook and Google than via any news organization in world history.[59] In addition to spreading actual news articles, social media also offer a unique opportunity to present self-images that reach broad publics.[60] Audiences have long been able to form close and intimate relationships with mediated characters at a distance.[61] Social media communication works in a very similar way as political candidates try to construct online personalities that audiences can relate to.[62] The goal is the audience's identification with the presented image. Yet the difference is the direct influence of the candidate on the constructed image. While politicians have always tried to influence their coverage in the media, here they are able to build their own image. At the same time, their level of control remains limited as they cannot fully control how the presented image is perceived. Social media image "disasters" still often occur, and the audience's reaction remains in many ways unpredictable.

Social media present a worldview in which connection and sharing are very desirable practices.[63] On Facebook you have to call people "friends" you have not seen for thirty years. Politicians are regularly taking advantage of this perception and illusion of personal "connection." Yet opportunities to successfully self-present on social media are not available to everyone on an equal basis. Studies have shown that female politicians are often cautious about self-personalization, while male politicians tend to see it as an opportunity to show a more humane image.[64] At least in the American context personalization does seem to work better for men. A survey of American voters showed that voters appreciated the personalized representation of male candidates regardless of which party the candidate belonged to, while they recognized the "increased presence" of personalized female candidates only if the candidates belonged to their own tribe.[65] The success of an authenticity performance will depend on many factors, some of which, even in the most professional campaigns, the performer cannot manipulate.

While social media campaigns are crucial components of contemporary political campaigns, they have not fully replaced more traditional forms of interactions with voting publics, such as rallies, knocking on doors, advertising, debates, and press conferences.[66] Performances of charm on social media are part of a larger information system,[67] where personal narratives and self-images travel across media platforms and offline worlds.

Charm as Weapon: The "Charm Offensive"

Charm can also be weaponized in the form of a "charm offensive." How can something be both endearing and militaristic? Charm offensives manage to do both. Charm offensives are public relations campaigns that weaponize the personal magnetism of political leaders, selected negotiators, or other representatives to radically shift a country's international image.[68] The charm of the politician is meant to appeal to a broad international audience with the hope of improving the country's brand. Because of the increased significance of political leaders and political personalization in shaping country images, tactful and relatable politicians can arrange rapid shifts in the perception of their countries. Magnetic personalities can help their country to be seen as trustworthy or even to become a source of inspiration for other countries.[69] Charm offensives, thus, have become key tools of nation branding.[70]

Charm offensives are connected to soft power, but these terms are not identical. While soft power is a marriage, a lasting commitment with ideally shared and memorable goals, charm offensive is a quick, powerful affair that captures hearts and is often forgotten quickly. Soft power, a term coined by political scientist Joseph Nye,[71] describes a public diplomacy in which a country enhances its international standing through its appealing value system. Soft power rests on three key resources: culture, political values, and foreign policies.[72] Soft power builds on "an attraction to shared values and the justness and duty of contributing to the achievement of those values."[73] In contrast, charm offensives do not assume the existence of any common values. They do not aspire to build any value systems. Charm offensives operate through visual appearance and sometimes through sensory deception. They are concerted image campaigns waged in a variety of forms and on a diversity of platforms from traditional mass media to social media. Charm offensives create momentary alliances, temporary new constellations that help achieve a foreign policy goal without necessarily building on or constructing any moral foundations.

In the American press, the term "charm offensive" was first mentioned in 1956 in connection with the Soviet Union.[74] At that time, the Soviet Union was branding itself as a modernizing empire. To showcase its progress to the wide world, it extended invitations to professionals, government officials, journalists, and other "influencers" to visit the Soviet Union on well-funded trips. This public diplomacy campaign worried many in the West, who saw it as a deceptive charm offensive. When Soviet tanks invaded Hungary in October 1956 to crush a revolution, the charm offensive swiftly ended as Western news publications condemned the Soviet actions on their front pages.[75]

In the 1960s and 1970s, the term was barely mentioned in the American press. "Charm offensive" again became popular in the mid-1980s to describe political transformations in the Soviet Union. It has been increasingly popular with American journalists ever since. On any given day, when readers open the *New York Times*, they are likely to find at least one foreign affairs article mentioning a charm offensive. Why is "charm offensive" so popular with American journalists today? There is no easy answer to that question as there are many pieces to the puzzle. Reasons range from the prevalence of political personalization to shrinking space for foreign affairs reporting in newspapers triggering spectacular coverage.

Politicians may or may not be good at performing personal magnetism in their everyday interactions, but charm offensives as campaigns construct relatable, "charming" features for the leader and communicate these features to local and international audiences. In some cases, charm offensives offer substitutes or proxies for leaders, such as members of their families or their close advisers to seduce the international audience. While charm offensives can be used even when a country is popular, most often they do not start from a neutral or positive standpoint. They are used to push a country's negative perception to a more positive level.

Charm offensives certainly existed before digital media (just think of the Soviet example), but they operate especially well in the current media environment that features a continuous transnational flow of visuals and texts and the ability for a global audience to respond instantaneously. Within this media ecology, contemporary charm offensives tend to focus on visual appearance, and sometimes on sensory deception. The charm offensive's initiators must provide events and sites that make good visuals for the international media to cover. When visual and textual representations of leaders instantaneously shape their countries' images, charm offensives seem to be key strategies of public diplomacy. With the help of a charm offensive, country leaders directly set some of the parameters of their media coverage, potentially shifting long-held public assumptions about their nations.

Countries can have "negative soft power," a strong negative reputation that can limit their ability to lead on the global stage.[76] Once a country has established negative soft power, it often faces extraordinary challenges in changing its international image. When the international audience reads a news story about a country that has negative soft power, it is already influenced by a negative bias. An image makeover thus does not start from a neutral point; it has to counter a very strong negative assumption.[77] In this case achieving fusion is particularly challenging and involves a process of "normalizing" the feared country in public opinion. Of course, even countries with a relatively favorable image can employ strategic public relations campaigns to boost their global reputation.

Charm offensives' primary audiences are not local; they are aimed at the public opinion of international audiences. While in previous, predigital media environments it was sometimes possible for politicians to focus exclusively on local audiences and direct their messages toward their professional foreign diplomatic counterparts, engaging with foreign publics is now an essential, almost unavoidable feature of diplomacy. This shift in diplomatic practices has happened in conjunction with rapid changes in the general media environment that enable more direct communication with foreign publics through social media.[78] Any utterance of a political leader can instantaneously travel in a complex web of global platforms, making it increasingly challenging to limit a message geographically. Diplomacy no longer happens exclusively between governments, nor is it limited to direct engagement between governments and citizens. Political leaders are well aware of this cultural and technological shift and often direct their messages to multiple local and international audiences.[79]

Contemporary charm offensives have three key features: (1) they focus on visual spectacle and public performance; (2) they place a political leader's image at the center of attention in contrast to other elements of the country's image; and (3) they operate particularly well in digital media environments that enable the quick and interactive dissemination of visual and textual information. Charm offensives have a brief time frame and relatively clear outcomes.

Journalists and politicians often discuss charm offensives with a language of admiration and surprise but can also use "charm offensive" as a derogatory term to condemn the intrusion of nonrationality and affect in politics.[80] Charm offensives are often mentioned critically by those who see them as a form of manipulation and deception that countries employ to hide their true intentions. The news media regularly cover charm offensives with a skeptical tone, highlighting the deceptive features of these campaigns, while enthusiastically showing the related spectacular scenes. Still, even if journalists discuss charm offensives in a skeptical tone, they find themselves covering these strategic campaigns, giving a platform to controversial leaders and their strategic public relations messages.

In sum, *charm* and *charm offensive* have emerged as keywords of contemporary global politics. Traditional forms of charisma centered on distanced leaders relying on rhetorically powerful speeches. These charismatic performances still occasionally occur and can be the basis for political success. But a distinctively different form of personal magnetism is increasingly present: charm. The charm of contemporary politicians is based on a perceived closeness or even intimacy with their audiences. We perceive the preferred politician as "one of our tribe" even though we most likely will never meet in person.

Charm is a nimble performance, a magical spell of authenticity and relatability in global, fragmented, and highly visual media. In this media environment, audiences have the illusion of directly communicating with their political leaders. Politicians pretend to lift the curtain and allow their followers to enter the backstage. They often drop their official mask to appear as our next-door neighbor who we can even have a beer with. Politicians also create minor and major events for the media, putting on enchanting fireworks for viewers. The spectacular and vulnerable performance of authenticity is at the core of charm, as politicians struggle to appear as one of us, while their jobs and lifestyles have little to do with the everyday circumstances of most of us. As we put increasing focus on individuals instead of institutions, our political ideals and futures are subject to a fast-changing array of political actors on the world stage. Charm can capture hearts and end divisions, but it can also be used to destroy fragile institutions and values. Charm is weaponized in fast-paced charm offensives to achieve short-term political goals, often by the "dark side."

Without understanding how seductive personalities rise to power, attract attention in new media, and then often fall, we cannot grasp the fragile political times we live in. In order to understand twenty-first-century politics, we have to grapple with the power of charm as it shapes the future of democracy worldwide.

2

Liberal Charm

NEW ZEALAND PRIME MINISTER JACINDA ARDERN

On June 23, 2018, prime minister of New Zealand Jacinda Ardern posted a Facebook live video with her newborn in her arms. With makeup properly applied, dressed in white, she just wanted to charmingly "check in" with her audience before putting the baby in the car seat. While no doubt carefully crafted, the video felt like a casual stop-by. She thanked her supporters and signaled that even with a baby in arms she is still hard at work! Ardern shared a wide array of similarly informal posts over her years as prime minister from 2017 until 2023. She provided followers with VIP access to both her personal life and her delicate political decisions. With cell phone in selfie mode most of the time, she shared high and low, both in feelings and in quality of imagery. While listening to her, many fans felt connected, listened to, and ultimately special. There is a particular feeling of being cared for in an environment where vulnerability is a feature not a bug.

The posts seemed natural, but they were anything but. Carefully constructed, they promoted a leader whose personal charm shone through. She was humble, present, dedicated, warm, and more than anything, "kind." In these videos we experienced the dramatic breakthrough of personality, a "charm attack" on viewers through a global distribution platform. Clearly the challenge Ardern faced was how to transport offline ideals, traditions, and practices of charm to online audiences. Every step of the way, she also navigated restrictive gender norms and expectations. Ultimately, by January 2023, the expectations became too much to carry, and Ardern announced her resignation. In a characteristic speech that emphasized the "person" even in the official role of the "prime minister," she said, "Politicians are human. We give all that we can for as long as we can. And then it's time. And for me, it's time."[1] Mourning Ardern's departure from politics, many were trying to understand her unique approach to public life. This chapter looks at the online construction of her personal charm.

While already active on Facebook in 2013, Ardern really hit it off from August 2017, when she built up a distinct digital persona with around ten posts a week. She prioritized Facebook over other forms of social media—she barely tweeted, and her Instagram was mostly a replication of her Facebook content. Facebook's affordances with longer posts and a combined focus on text and imagery seemed to better suit her relatively nuanced messaging. In 2021, Facebook was also the most popular platform in New Zealand, with two-thirds of New Zealanders having a profile on the site. Ardern sometimes gave priority to her Facebook page even over other forms of messaging available to a state leader; she sometimes presented her newest ad campaigns on Facebook first, before moving it to national television, offering her audience a certain sense of special access.

Ardern's most popular topics were the environment, health, labor, indigenous concerns, child poverty, and housing issues. But from time to time she also threw some "quotidian" events into the mix: struggle with balancing work and motherhood, organizing her paperwork, feeling exhausted, wearing a hoodie. She took pride in introducing topics that humanized her and created waves of communication. A key example was the very public discussion of her infertility and then finally achieved pregnancy.

She also designed events that would attract interest and create bonding. In a particularly famous instance, Ardern took her small baby along to her 2018 speech at the UN General Assembly. The event offered an occasion to comment on everyday aspects of motherhood (where would you change a diaper in a UN building?). Ardern not only performed as an "authentic" politician—she was strategically maneuvering to establish legitimacy through charm in form and content, especially at times when her authority was contested. Knowing that her gender and motherhood would influence her public perception, she was consciously using these qualities to preempt attacks, attract attention, and create connection. When her ability to juggle multiple public and private responsibilities was questioned, she would make sure to forefront this dilemma in her posts in an endearing and performative way, controlling the messaging from upfront.

In her regular community check-ins on Facebook, we could see and hear her, but the interaction lacked many of the defining features of everyday charming interactions. How could she make the viewer feel the "one and only" when she had millions of viewers in fragmented international settings? How could she look into your eyes, offer reflection, develop connection? A few of her key strategies of embracing and performing charm stand out.

Being Always There for You—Performing the Authentic Caregiver

Jacinda Ardern's performative projection of "authentic caring" started right at the beginning of her videos. She had a habit of opening her Facebook videos in an informal, hugging tone: "Hey, just wanted to jump online to check in with you all" or "kia ora ["be healthy" in Maori], everyone!" and frequently ended the "interaction" with "talk soon" or "take care."[2] The foundational video mentioned before that established her tone and remains her most viewed video to this day, was a video she took while leaving the hospital with her newborn. In what would become classic Ardern style, she started the video with "hi everyone, this will be a super quick one as we are just loading up the car and getting ready to leave Oakland Hospital." She also quickly emphasized: "I didn't want to leave the hospital without saying thank you."[3] The video did not have a particular political content in the strict sense, with no policy decisions or announcements to share. It was truly a community "check-in" at a major turning point of her life, which also directly addressed some people's gendered concerns about whether she would manage it all.

Of course, the visual announcement of a birth has a long tradition, most famously among royal family members in the United Kingdom. But it also has a somewhat sacred quality, reflected, for instance in the "scandal" around Prince Harry's and Meghan Markle's refusal to follow tradition in this context and rather protect their privacy. Ardern, dropping much of the glamor and secrecy around this moment, brought the viewers right into the room where she recovered with her partner and baby after birth. Doing so she constructed intimacy, but also communicated a persistent, never-ceasing ethic of always being on stage. She stated that there was indeed no boundary between work and personal life, and her personality and personhood.

This persistent entanglement of work and private life was also reinforced by her partner's tweets. Being a professional television entertainer, Ardern's partner, Clarke Gayford, clearly knew how to build up anticipation around events. Two days before the birth of their baby, Gayford tweeted: "Anyone with aspirations of being PM, make sure you also have an appetite for reading and reading and reading and reading. #stillwaiting." The tweet was accompanied by a photo of pregnant Ardern leaning over a small coffee table, surrounded by piles of work papers (fig. 2.1). While she persistently communicated "care" to the audience, there seemed to be a strong disconnect when she presented her relentless work. In her authenticity performance, there was little care or protection for herself, other than acknowledging the community that supports her. While the "hard-work" images were often presented ironically and in a self-deprecating manner, ultimately they did communicate a rather harsh work ethic and adhered to unrealistic expectations toward women in leadership roles. The message seemed to entail: "I work extremely hard so that I can care for you."

The message of caring was woven into a wide variety of posts. Posting about her meeting with kids, for instance, she said:

Clarke Gayford
@NZClarke

Anyone with aspirations of being PM, make sure you also have an appetite for reading and reading and reading and reading. #stillwaiting

9:25 PM · Jun 19, 2018

FIG. 2.1. Posted by Jacinda Ardern's partner, Clarke Gayford, on Twitter, June 19, 2018.

Today when I asked "what's our job in parliament?" One
of the children's hands shot up "keeping people safe."
And that's so true! But we talked a little bit about what
looking after people means, and how important it is that
we try and look after our minds too, no matter how young
or old we are.[4]

Kids were often interlocutors in Ardern's posts as she frequently presented herself in a special "public motherhood"
role.

This culture of performative care in small-scale contexts where personal charm had a chance to shine was then
extrapolated to national events and global politics. In her
first speech to the UN General Assembly, Ardern argued: "If
I could distill it down into one concept that we are pursuing
in New Zealand, it is simple and it is this: kindness."[5] She said
this at a time when there was a particular longing for icons of
kindness to counter the very masculine presidential culture
promoted by then US president Trump. Every utterance of
kindness and display of a diplomatic smile appeared as a
rebuke of the culture of "America First!"[6]

Perhaps no other example illustrated Ardern's global
message of kindness more than her internationally acclaimed
response to the Christchurch terrorist attack. In March 2019,
an Australian white supremacist opened fire in two mosques
in Christchurch, New Zealand. He killed fifty-one people
and injured forty, while livestreaming the murders on Facebook. The visuals of the attack were thus aired on the same
platform as Ardern's persistent messaging of kindness. Ardern, in her very first public statement, called the attacks the
"darkest days of New Zealand," marked by an "extraordinary and unprecedented act of violence." She immediately

drew a line between "us" (New Zealanders) and "them" (the attacker), rebutting the othering of the Muslim minority:

> Many of those who will have been directly affected by this shooting may be migrants to New Zealand, they may even be refugees here. They have chosen to make New Zealand their home, and it is their home. They are us. The person who has perpetuated this violence against us is not.[7]

Demonstratively wearing a black head scarf, Ardern then traveled to Christchurch the next day. Her images, hugging Muslim men, women, and children, and projecting a personal aura of kindness, traveled around the globe. "New Zealand mourns with you, we are one," she emphasized in a speech, but more than words, her hugs expressed the message: we belong to the same community. Throughout the visit, she was performatively deconstructing walls and barriers between religious communities. Her personal charm was at the foreground; the power of personality rose above all dividing ideologies and convictions. Personality was not a sidebar; it was presented as the ultimate solution to overcome division.

Three days after the attacks, Ardern gave a powerful speech in Parliament. Opening with "Salam alaikum. Peace be upon you and peace be upon all of us," she promised not to utter the name of the attacker in order to deprive him of the "notoriety" he sought. Again, she repeated that all victims were "New Zealanders, they are us. Because they are us, we as a nation, mourn them. We feel a huge duty of care to them." Note the language of care made explicit and bold. She also honored the first responders. Later, regarding the ongoing trial, she stated that the families of the fallen would receive justice. Addressing the role of social media in disseminating extremist content, she argued that "there cannot be a case of all profit, no responsibility." She closed with, again, "We are one, they are us. Ko Tatou Tatou ["We are one" in Maori]. Salam alaikum."[8]

Ardern's relatable iconography and vocabulary of "kindness" and "caring" was picked up by many worldwide. People replicated the imagery in sculptures, murals, and drawings. Perhaps the most striking representation appeared in Melbourne, Australia. After a quick and successful online fund-raising, street artist Loretta Lizzio painted a mural on a twenty-five-meter-tall silo. The mural shows Ardern embracing a Muslim woman in the wake of the Christchurch shooting (fig. 2.2). The same image was also projected onto the world's tallest building, the Burj Khalifa in Dubai, highlighting the global reach of the Ardern iconography (fig. 2.3). Her message of kindness traveled around the world, showcasing a new form of political performance in times of terrorism and gun violence.

Demasking—Daring to Be Vulnerable

Ardern's charm was performed through vulnerability and imperfection. She seemed to particularly enjoy poorly staged photographs, low-quality audio, and above all the "charm" of awkwardness.

In early 2021, in the middle of a global pandemic, she invited her Facebook audience to a press conference on New Zealand's climate goals. Ardern opened the video in her usual casual style: "Hi there, just thought you might wanna join us," and then handed over the phone to her press secretary, who recorded the complete press conference that they then walked into, but without a proper microphone. A particularly endearing part of the video was an endless

FIG. 2.2. Mural of Ardern in Melbourne. Photo by Stuart Holdsworth (www.inspiringcity.com).

HH Sheikh Mohammed ✓
@HHShkMohd

⋯

New Zealand today fell silent in honour of the mosque attacks' martyrs. Thank you PM @jacindaardern and New Zealand for your sincere empathy and support that has won the respect of 1.5 billion Muslims after the terrorist attack that shook the Muslim community around the world.

سلام
peace

12:08 PM · Mar 22, 2019

FIG. 2.3. Posted by Prime Minister of the United Arab Emirates Mohammed bin Rashid Al Maktoum (@Hhshkmohd) on Instagram, March 22, 2019.

walk-through in a rather drab-looking office building, until they finally reached the press conference room. The backstage became the frontstage, and charm and expertise shone through technical difficulties. Ardern turned the idea of the press conference upside down, giving the central significance to social media. Here again she emphasized the importance of accidental and imperfect "backstages" in public life.[9]

Ardern also often enjoyed mistakes. In a video on February 5, 2021, she used the wrong camera function. Instead of pointing at her, the camera captured a giant trash can and a couple of bored policemen. Ardern, visibly pleased by the failure, started the video with a huge smile, followed by a quick apology: "Sorry, started in the wrong direction!" After that, wearing a Maori necklace, she showed the viewer around the traditional celebration where government officials barbecued for guests to celebrate the national public holiday Waitangi Day.[10]

Other times she took delight in trivializing major diplomatic events. In one video, wearing an old, gray hoodie, looking tired, talking about a long list of activities, she happened to mention her first phone call with US president-elect Joe Biden. As she was recording the video live, one viewer asked whether she was indeed wearing a hoodie. Ardern quickly responded, "I can assure you that my attire will not negatively affect that work [referring to her coronavirus pandemic response]."[11] Similarly casual videos showed her "checking in" with the late Queen Elizabeth or giving a talk at the UN. Here her public and private persona were blurred, as she moved from one role to the next. Surprised comments under her posts revealed how much she was pushing gender walls just by wearing a hoodie or daring to look tired. Her defensive commentary highlighted the absurd standards she was subjected to.

She also laughed off attacks, relaxing tense situations. A primary example was a controversial interview conducted by the American television show *60 Minutes*. The interviewer commented on Ardern's attractiveness and asked a series of inappropriate questions. One question particularly shocked her social media fans: "There is one really important political question I want to ask you, and that is, what exactly is the date the baby's due?" As the scandal unfolded, Ardern seemed to be unshaken by the interview: "Maybe it's just that I'm from Morrinsville. I don't know. I just wasn't particularly fazed by any of it" (Morrinsville is a small town on New Zealand's North Island where Ardern grew up).[12] This shrugging off was a very performative gesture that left little space for critique, but also opened up space to "move on."

The message of imperfection was also communicated through her repetition in outfits. Ardern almost never changed during a day. She wore the same outfit to visit a school and give a press conference and then did a live video. The outfits were recognizable over time and sent the conscious message of "I am working hard; I am not interested in questions about appearance." All these examples coalesced around the idea of vulnerability, imperfection, and relatability in a highly gendered context. They endeared, attracted, and ultimately charmed many members of Ardern's audience. These were all examples of her attempts to "demask," to move beyond the rigid, formal role of a professional politician, and to carve out a special role as a female politician on the global stage.

Equalizing—Fusion with the "Team of Five Million"

One of the key strategies of Ardern's performative charm is to homogenize the audience to achieve fusion. How would you build community with "faceless" strangers online? One method seems to be shared activities. In the middle of the coronavirus pandemic in February 2021, Ardern decided to mobilize her Facebook fans around finding a toy bunny's owner (fig. 2.4). The bunny had been lost at a busy airport several months earlier. She "quickly" posted:

> I think everyone who has a little person in their lives will know how important these precious things can be, so maybe you can help us find whoever "wink" belongs to? (NB I think "wink" has only acquired a name, safety jacket, mask and ID since living at the airport . . . hopefully that won't stop it being recognised!)

She invoked the image of a close-knit village where everybody knows each other to create fusion with a diverse and international Facebook "community," whose "members" most likely have never met. For this community, no task was too small, and emotional investment was a must. The image was again highly gendered, as she is presented as the ultimate mother of the nation, exhibiting caring and compassion.

Another example is Ardern's frequent invention of contests or competitions. She once initiated a Christmas card design competition, inviting young people to send their creative illustrations to her. She later updated people on the contest and ultimately announced the winners. This direct care and performance gave the sense of an "open government," of two-way communication within a charming interaction.

She also triggered community fusion by enthusiastically commenting on incoming letters. During the 2020 coronavirus pandemic, she shared the letter of a child who was complaining about her Dad's habits:

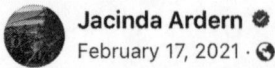

Jacinda Ardern ✔
February 17, 2021 · 🌐

Landed in Hamilton this morning and the airport team kindly let me use their board room for a couple of meetings. As I was leaving they introduced me to this wee bunny. It was found at the airport on the 28th of January and they've been looking for its owner ever since! I think everyone who has a little person in their lives will know how important these precious things can be, so maybe you can help us find whoever "wink" belongs to? (NB I think "wink" has only acquired a name, safety jacket, mask and ID since living at the airport....hopefully that won't stop it being recognised!)

👍❤️ 49K   2.3K 💬   4K ➤

👍 Like   💬 Comment

FIG. 2.4. Posted by Jacinda Ardern on Facebook, January 17, 2021.

Going through letters when I came across this. "Jacinda. My dad is not washing his hands properly. He is not putting soap on his hands and rubbing for twenty seconds. I will work on this with him." Love the offer of support right at the end there. ☺[13]

The pandemic put Ardern in a particularly challenging position. She needed to communicate strict community rules, while preserving her general message of kindness and generosity. Nothing would have been further from Ardern than a "dictator role" that weaponized authoritarian communication without compassion, understanding, and complexity. She always looked for the delicate balance between clear messaging and human warmth. Through the child's note she broadcast strong public health messages, but without an authoritarian tone. By her selection of letters and astute commentary, she communicated values in an indirect way. Especially through children, Ardern projected a community being built every single day through performative acts of kindness and support.

Charming her followers as "one" community took considerable effort. She often spoke about "we," or a "team of five million New Zealanders," especially in the context of trying to tackle the 2020 pandemic "together." She frequently opened and closed her Facebook live videos in Maori and had a special focus on indigenous issues. The immediate reaction to Christchurch with the message of "they are us" was another example of her creating a strong, integrative identity of an open, but also affective patriotism. In all these cases, charm worked as a method to collapse walls and project an imagined community.

Restaging—Finding New Sites of Political Interaction

Jacinda Ardern's charm was performed in well-selected locations. In other words, she had a great emphasis on the "stage" of the charming interaction. She often made the stage more visible by highlighting its evident failures. A regular ritual was her apology for the setting she appeared in. On February 11, 2021, she used the backseat of a car to announce the arrival of the first coronavirus vaccines.[14] At the video's beginning she immediately apologized for recording in the car, pointing out that she did not have any other gap in her tightly packed schedule. Again, the usual press procedure was neglected in favor of direct and personal communication. She framed Facebook live videos as her prime obligation while apologizing for the setting, in effect presenting a stage or mise-en-scène in disguise. She also regularly emphasized the imperfectness of the stage in response to audience questions. In one video, when asked about the reasons for being tired, she mentioned sitting next to her newborn's diaper pail. Similar examples of unusual stages, or the failure of the stage, flooded her Facebook site, making one wonder what the actual function of these site selections was. Backstage was practically gone; everything appeared on the frontal, visible, transparent main stage. Imperfect performances constructed a more vulnerable, relatable character, who cast her magic spell through her love for the "everyday."

Ardern's Global Charm

It is easy to assume that Ardern had a coherent national and international image. But this was strikingly not the case.

While her local image centered on vulnerability, the global image projected an iconic and glamorous anti-Trump figure. Powerful examples include her image on the cover of the British edition of *Vogue*, the announcement that she was among *Time* magazine's top one hundred most influential persons in 2019, and a series of opinion makers and influencers declaring her their role model, an icon, or, even a "political prodigy."[15] London's mayor in his laudatory remarks in *Time* magazine summarized Ardern's key messages:

> Jacinda Ardern's leadership since the attack has been an inspiration to us all. Not only is she delivering such swift action on gun control, she has sent a powerful message around the world about our shared values—that those who seek to divide us will never succeed, and that New Zealand will always protect and celebrate the diversity and openness that make our countries so great.[16]

Note the abstractness of the ideals. They are strong values and policies, far removed from the everydayness and charm of Ardern's daily online communication.

Ardern also often pops up as an example of ideal leadership. Perhaps the most succinct summary came from Oprah Winfrey: "I've never seen such leadership," Winfrey said to an exuberant audience at the Women of the World Summit in 2019 in New York, adding that Ardern set a "global standard in leadership" by projecting "peace and goodness." Oprah concluded that "we need to make the choice, every single day—to channel our own inner Jacindas, with the aim to exemplify the truth, and the respect and the grace that we actually wish for the world."[17] Applauding Ardern's response to the Christchurch shooting, *Psychology Today* also argued: "As her nation heals, Ardern has shown that a focus on what perhaps some have disparaged as overly soft values to emphasize in leadership are actually powerful strengths: kindness, sympathy, love."[18] Again, commentators picked up on her message of kindness, but her messages of vulnerability, mistakes, and accidents were left behind in the international, more abstract interpretation.

In all these representations, there is one binding feature: Jacinda Ardern took on the role of the anti-Trump icon of kindness in global politics and culture. Her rise as a global icon was strongly tied to the shifting image of the United States during the Trump administration. Some commentators made the contrast explicit. The title of an article in *Vogue* (February 14, 2018) said it all: "New Zealand's Prime Minister, Jacinda Ardern, Is Young, Forward-Looking, and Unabashedly Liberal—Call Her the Anti-Trump." The related image featured her in a top-model pose, photographed at a beautiful beach near Auckland, New Zealand. She radiated power, beauty—something of an alternate reality for liberal readers in a faraway country, presented only through stereotypes. The message was clear: a different type of politics is possible. Through a highly gendered, condensed, and simplified representation, an ideal icon was built up.

This is in some ways the opposite of the charming interaction Jacinda performed "at home." This global icon is stripped of complexity, nuance, and contradiction. Perhaps the most striking example of the clash of Jacinda as the "humble" performer in New Zealand and the global anti-Trump icon was her actual meeting with her iconized image. How so? At one point she posted an image to Facebook in which she actually met "herself" (fig. 2.5). The photo showed a woman sitting on a plane turning back and wearing a facemask with Ardern's portrait as a pattern. Flight attendants giggled in the background. Ardern commented: "still laughing." The natural gesture of turning around to say good morning underlined the spontaneity and authenticity of this shot and triggered a record number of likes.

On Facebook, playing with her own icon is something of a pastime for Ardern. A striking example included her commentary on a vandalized campaign image, which showed her with horns and black teeth. She seemed to take pleasure in making ironic comments about the image, signaling the ability to "touch" and redefine her icon. By clashing and slashing her global icon with ironic commentary, she seemingly took down the icon, but in fact made it even stronger.[19] Another example was her reaction to the oversized Melbourne mural of her hugging a member of the Muslim community after the Christchurch attacks. Ardern quickly commented: "I'm humbled by it, though, because obviously what happened in Christchurch for me will always be about the Muslim community that it happened to. It didn't happen to me."[20] She tried to refocus the conversation, but this commentary also created another news cycle for the Ardern mural.

In her Facebook community, Ardern frequently contrasted her idealized, simplified, and condensed political icon with a "real," charming, and vulnerable everyday self. Both of course were highly constructed and astutely performed. Overall, Ardern's central challenge was to bring audiences closer, to replicate the magic of charm in diffused and fragmented media environments. She worked hard on performing personal, individualized connections. She also struggled with what Sarah Banet-Weiser termed "popular feminism"[21]—a type of feminism that is attractive, performative, and widely accepted, without the political controversy of traditional political feminism or postfeminism's neglect of

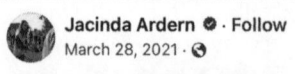

When the person in front of you on the plane turns around to say good morning...still laughing 😂

FIG. 2.5. "When the person in front of you on the plane turns around to say good morning . . . still laughing." Posted by Jacinda Ardern on Facebook, March 28, 2021.

contemporary discriminatory practices. Ardern was react-
ing to expectations and looked for a moderate solution,
without an attempt to change the expectations. She consciously performed expected "humble" attitudes in contrast
to her global rock-star image. She charmed in everyday-style
interaction and in playful attempts to attack and reaffirm her
global image.

3

Illiberal Charm

HUNGARIAN PRIME MINISTER VIKTOR ORBÁN

With some resignation on his face, one of Viktor Orbán's long-term acquaintances said, "He has incredible charisma about him, he's a real politician. I hate the things Orbán represents now, but each time I see him, I feel that attraction to him again. I can't draw myself out of this magic spell."[1] Those who regularly meet him tend to have a similar assessment. Hungarian prime minister Viktor Orbán makes you feel yourself to be the only one in the room. He pays attention, charms, and seduces as he pleases. The media also love to pick up on this quality. *The Times* called the Hungarian prime minister a "charismatic and ruthless political operator,"[2] the *Atlantic* described him as "full of charisma, ambition and tactical skill,"[3] and the *Guardian* noted that Orbán's success is not all down to authoritarian ruthlessness: "there is also warmth and charm when required."[4]

Viktor Orbán's looks do not make him a likely candidate for a charming leader. He is short; in recent years has gained significant weight; he is famously clueless about fashion and even proud of having no idea how to use basic contemporary technologies. In some sense, he is every political stylist's worst nightmare. But Orbán has won four elections in a row by big margins, and despite his controversial policies he is much admired and supported by many in Hungary and beyond. He is the most reelected prime minister in the history of Hungarian politics. It is a commonplace among Hungarian political analysts that Viktor Orbán's brand is much stronger than his party's. His movement is based on him as an individual, and in case of his untimely death, many think his party would be unlikely to recover.[5]

Orbán was already described as charismatic in 1989, widely celebrated in the West as the political hope for the country's transition to democracy. He gave a powerful speech at the reburial of Prime Minister Imre Nagy, leader of the 1956 Hungarian Revolution against the Soviets, who was executed after the revolution. In his speech, Orbán firmly urged the withdrawal of Soviet troops from Hungary. This speech catapulted him to local and international political prominence. Orbán first became prime minister in 1998, leading a center-right government until 2002. By this time, he was the most powerful political figure of his party, Fidesz (Alliance of Young Democrats), establishing a culture in which voting for Fidesz meant voting for Orbán.[6]

During the first Orbán government, the Office of the Prime Minister became the central point of political power.[7] Though this process of centralization was mirrored by other political parties in Hungary and the larger region, it was most pronounced in Hungary.[8] The Hungarian government also started to occupy the public service broadcasters and some independent media outlets.[9] Yet, Orbán suffered two election losses in 2002 and 2006 from left-liberal prime minister candidate Ferenc Gyurcsány, cementing his view that stronger interventions and a more favorable media environment would be needed to secure a win and keep power in the future.[10] Fidesz won the elections in 2010 and almost immediately changed the constitution—a set of sweeping legal changes and a firm grip on the media sphere followed. In 2014, Fidesz won again more than two-thirds of the seats in the Parliament and has remained the dominant political force in the country ever since.

Using Fidesz's solid parliamentary majority, in 2018 a government-friendly media foundation was established, and it has become the most significant player in the Hungarian media market, effectively capturing it. In just a few hours, the foundation became the largest media company in Hungary as many government-friendly media owners freely gifted their properties to the new entity. The foundation owns media companies, TV and radio stations, newspapers, magazines, and news websites.[11] These outlets now present a very controlled and coordinated image of the government, often even publishing the very same front pages. Some oppositional news outlets and channels, particularly online, are still active, but they operate with significant financial limitations given the government's influence on the advertising market.

Many populist politicians use social media to circumvent mass media that they cannot control, a primary example of the practice being Trump. This is not the case for Viktor Orbán. Given his extensive direct control of the local mass

media landscape, including the public service broadcasters, use of social media is only one of his many effective
communication platforms. In the international context
the situation is slightly different. Orbán perceives Western
media outlets as hostile and turns to social media as a tool
to counter and circumvent the Western narratives that are
often critical of him.

When considering the popularity of illiberalism worldwide, we often focus on media capture, on the ways in
which illiberal and populist leaders gain control over
independent media outlets. But it is equally important to
understand how leaders capture hearts through a well-
constructed image, especially on social media. Orbán
dramatically outpaces other Hungarian politicians on
Facebook, the dominant platform in Hungary, clocking in
nearly 1.2 million followers (Hungary has a population of
close to ten million). Fidesz officials were convinced that
the 2022 elections would in fact be decided on Facebook.[12]
A new Orbán "brand" was introduced in 2021, with a recognizable logo and the colors of red, white, and green (the
colors of the Hungarian flag). With frequent simultaneous
translation into English, Orbán's Facebook site attempts to
portray him as an international player in the transnational
network of illiberalism. In October 2022, Orbán also joined
the social media platform Twitter[13]—in his first post he
asked why his "good friend," Donald Trump, was not there
anymore (Trump at that time was banned from Twitter).
Given that Twitter was not popular in Hungary, this was
clearly a way to communicate to a global audience and
gather international attention, while also keeping his Facebook and Instagram accounts. Orbán is also active on the
video-hosting service TikTok, where his content targets

younger audiences, for instance in the form of Star Wars–themed videos that present his politics as a fight against the dark side.

Orbán's international image in Western liberal media is that of a "strongman,"[14] a bully, effectively a fascist "mini-Mussolini." But his social media image shows a more nuanced and complicated personality that frequently exhibits a certain type of illiberal and populist charm. His image includes elements ranging from a relentless fighter to a gentle protector to a populist politician who is nonetheless frolicking in elite, professional politics. But overall, despite twists and turns in opinions and policies, Orbán appears as a symbolic condensation of the nation, marking the nation's boundaries and deciding who is allowed to belong, and who is ultimately excluded. This chapter looks at the strategic construction of his political persona on Facebook.

Equalizing the Audience and Drawing the Boundaries of the Nation

Orbán uses many methods to allude to the nation and to position himself as its iconic representation. A particularly popular method is referring to meals and pastries that are understood to be "quintessentially Hungarian." During the 2022 campaign, Orbán frequently visited pastry shops and food carts selling *lángos*, a type of fried bread popular in the country. These visits were recorded in a batch of photographs and videos in which he highlighted his deep familiarity with these food items by ruminating on which type or topping to get (fig. 3.1). The nation was evoked and imagined, often indirectly. Yet even his subtle allusions to the nation, such as sampling pastries before Christmas, clearly signal the

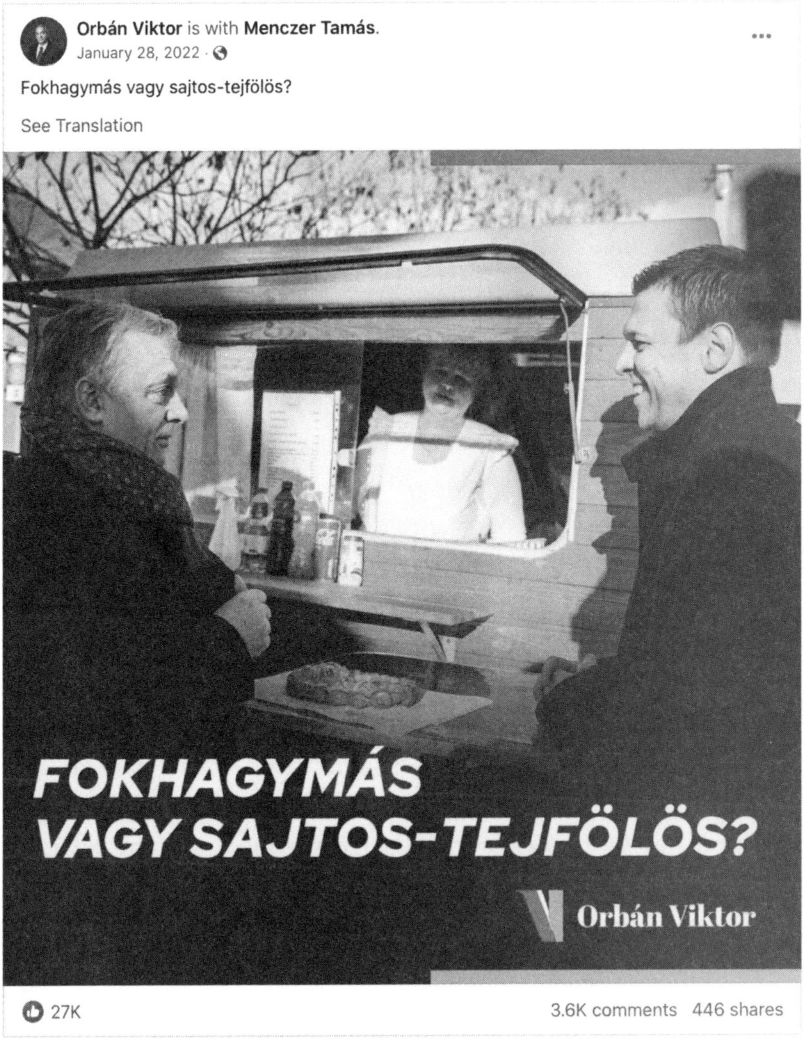

Orbán Viktor is with **Menczer Tamás**.
January 28, 2022 · 🌐

Fokhagymás vagy sajtos-tejfölös?

See Translation

FOKHAGYMÁS VAGY SAJTOS-TEJFÖLÖS?

V Orbán Viktor

FIG. 3.1. "Garlic or cheese-and-sour-cream?" Posted by Viktor Orbán on Facebook, January 28, 2022.

message of Christianity. Seemingly banal moments link to the larger values he aims to communicate.

A particular powerful example was his participation in a pig slaughter, a popular pastime in the Hungarian countryside. In a characteristic photograph, Orbán stood in front of the slaughtered, upside-down pig, staring into the future, almost evoking the famous "Hope" Obama image in a somewhat absurd context (fig. 3.2). The headline stated "after a hard fight." The image presented his fighter image, connected him to Hungarian tradition, and yet highlighted him as "one of us," a member of the community. He referred to the nation in a subtle way without referencing it directly. The image was blurred, with one recognizable character in the center: Viktor Orbán.

Clearly, his "one of us" image was not targeting the urban intelligentsia. While participating in a folk tradition, Orbán alluded to his understanding of the nation as being built on tradition, without making this reference explicit. The headline referred to both his ongoing international "fights" and his fateful election campaign in 2022. Yet, it is worth noting what he did not refer to: high culture. Hungary has a strong international reputation for art, classical music, science, mathematics, and literature, but these cultural features rarely become part of Orbán's rendering of Hungarian tradition, perhaps because many of these high-cultural events happen in the country's capital, Budapest, a city that remains an oppositional stronghold. The rare occasions when Orbán posts about intellectual achievements are mostly connected to awards Hungarians win, such as scientist Katalin Karikó's Nobel Prize in 2023.

Orbán also constructed the boundaries of the nation and the contours of his personality through posts that celebrate exceptional Hungarian athletic achievements or commemorate intellectuals, artists, and athletes who have

Orbán Viktor ✓
16 January 2022 · 🌐

···

Kemény küzdelem után

Ippon

Ⅴ Orbán Viktor

👍😆 43K   4.4K comments 667 shares

FIG. 3.2. "After a hard fight" / "Ippon" [referring to a full throw in Japanese martial arts, when the opponent lands on his back]. Posted by Viktor Orbán on Facebook, January 16, 2022.

recently passed away. The posts about sports mostly focus on soccer—Orbán's favorite sport, which he lavishly funds, as he tries to reinvigorate Hungary's former soccer glory.[15] The posts give a glimpse into who Orbán considers worth celebrating in Hungary. Only a few refer to an international figure, for instance when the Hungarian prime minister commemorated the passing of French actor Jean-Paul Belmondo, alluding to the action thriller "The Professional," where Belmondo starred as a secret agent settling scores.[16] Through these posts, Orbán appears as more approachable, as "one of us," rooting for the national team or expressing appreciation of selected artists in popular culture.

As political scientist Jan-Werner Müller has put it, populism is "an exclusionary form of identity politics."[17] Who is excluded is key to developing the boundary of the populist's intended community. As symbolic condensation of the nation, Orbán aims to draw the boundaries of "us" and "them" in his imagination of the community of "real Hungarians." The drawing of the nation's boundaries often occurs in indirect ways (sampling food, participating in rituals), but frequently also through direct attacks on a wide variety of enemies against whom, in Orbán's presented worldview, symbolic and actual walls must be erected. Orbán has frequently targeted the LGBTQ community and the "global gender lobby." He ran extended campaigns against Hungarian American philanthropist and financier George Soros, whose foundation sent Orbán on a fellowship to study at Oxford University in 1989. "Migrants" have remained his persistent targets since 2015, when mostly Syrian nationals traveled through the country to reach Western destinations. Orbán even erected a fence at the Hungarian borders against migrants, which is still a regular feature in his political campaigns. The fence as a symbol is meant to embody his success as a defender of the nation. The complex combination of direct attacks and subtle allusions to the nation form a powerful mix in his communication.

Restaging—Opening New Spaces of Engagement

Viktor Orbán often opens up his private sphere—his home and his family—to the cameras. This is a feature of his campaigns that is rarely known or acknowledged by international observers. In one of Orbán's popular Facebook photographs, he sits on a pink couch with his wife and grandchildren (fig. 3.3). The image is captioned "Grandpa is a man, grandma is a woman, and they should leave our grandchildren alone" ("they" referring to the LGBTQ community). Here the political message is tough and clear, and Orbán again appears in the image of a "protector." Yet the photograph is not a stock image. Rather, it is a highly personal introduction to Orbán's own grandchildren.

Recently, a new genre also emerged in Orbán's representation: selfies with his voters. Selfies work as a new "stage" for Orbán in his attempt to reach younger voters. This imagery is in direct contrast to his overall presentation as an old-school conservative politician. His manners, appearance, and preferences otherwise lean toward tradition, not reform. The selfie is thus a highly unusual rendering of Orbán, and he looks somewhat uncomfortable and even awkward in these images.

Both categories, inviting viewers to the politician's home and taking selfies with voters, are regularly used by contemporary politicians as strategies to charm. But Orbán is new to this game. His mediated image has always been highly controlled; these seemingly unpredictable moments to charm seem professional and manufactured. Still, based on

Orbán Viktor ✔ · Follow
2 April 2022 · 🌐

A nagypapa férfi, a nagymama nő, az unokáinkat meg hagyják békén!

👍❤️😮 52K   3.6K comments 1.2K shares

FIG. 3.3. "Grandpa is a man, grandma is a woman, and they should leave our grandchildren alone!" Posted by Viktor Orbán on Facebook, April 2, 2022.

his Facebook engagement numbers, many of his followers seem to appreciate these mundane moments in which Orbán appears as approachable, as relatable, as a modern "one of us."

Demasking—Orbán's Dual Identity on the Global and Local Stage

Orbán possesses a rather firm, confrontational, and assertive image in the international arena, which earned him the label "wannabe fascist" from fascism expert Federico

FIG. 3.4. "Happy Mother's Day!" Posted by Viktor Orbán on Facebook, May 2, 2021.

Finchelstein.[18] Yet on his personal Facebook profile he also performs a surprisingly gentle side. His constructed gentleness appears mostly in attentive interactions with voters, particularly with families. In a popular Facebook post, he helps a young father carry a stroller in which a toddler sleeps. The headline says in both English and Hungarian: "A Scout's duty is to help others."[19] In another photograph, he gives a warm hug to his mother on Mother's Day (fig. 3.4).

In another popular video, he greets a young, about-to-wed couple in the Budapest Castle area. Orbán apologizes for not having shaved, and he mentions that his grandkids smudged him with "pörköltszósz" (a Hungarian beef/pork stew), yet he comes to greet the couple. In another "gentle" image, he is taking care of one of his grandchildren over the weekend. The image is entitled "weekend shift."

His marked support for animals is also a new trope that became significant during the 2022 campaign. A series of posts announced that Orbán delivered food to animal shelters or expressed his disgust with animal torturers (fig. 3.5). These posts are surprising at first, but they fit neatly into his overall image of a protector in a wide variety of contexts in uncertain times. His 2022 anti-LGBTQ referendum was framed as a defense of minors. On posters that were widely distributed and presented in the country, the government argued that "we need to protect our children" (fig. 3.6)

Throughout these posts, the protector side of Orbán is repeatedly emphasized against a broad and odd array of "dangers" that he attempts to portray as similar—from animal torturers to the LGBTQ movement. Unlike Ardern's liberal politics of universal care, Orbán's caring is targeted as he draws the boundaries of "Hungarian-ness" every step of the way. His caring side embraces those inside and simultaneously excludes people who do not fit his preferred categories.

The Personal Appeal of Political Competence

A distinctive set of posts has highlighted Orbán's political competence. Unlike many other populist leaders, he emphasizes his strong skills in traditional elite politics.[20] This seems

Orbán Viktor ✓ · Follow
October 5, 2021 · 🌐

Hahó, facebookosok!

Újra itt. Az állatokra nem csak az állatok világnapján kell figyelni. Vigyázzunk rájuk! 😊

#alfi 🐱🐱🐱

See Translation

Vigyázzunk rájuk!

ÁLLATOK VILÁGNAPJA   ◥ Orbán Viktor

👍❤️ 10K   2.1K comments   761 shares

👍 Like   💬 Comment   ↪ Share

FIG. 3.5. "Hi Facebookers. I am here again. We have to pay attention to animals not only on World Animal Day. Let's protect them! #alfi" / "Let's protect them! World Animal Day." Posted by Viktor Orbán on Facebook, October 5, 2021.

FIG. 3.6. "Let's protect our children!" Government poster in Budapest, photo taken by Julia Sonnevend, April 2022.

to capture his double-agent political persona: on the one hand a skilled and experienced politician, on the other hand an international disruptor. For any other democratic politician, these posts would look standard and predictable. But given Orbán's global disruptor and troublemaker image, his emphasis on the traditional craft of politics is a feature worth mentioning.

While frequently attacking the European Union, Orbán often posts about his professional interactions within the same alliance. He deploys various strategies to blur this contradiction. Sometimes he posts videos where he explains the debates from his perspective. In a video entitled "Brussels wants to send LGBTQ activists to Hungarian schools. We will not let this happen!," he carefully frames the debate as happening between Orbán and Brussels. He does not name concrete partners in negotiations. But with the person of Orbán as a symbolic condensation of Hungary, we have a clearly contoured fighter on the other side. This framing also often magnifies Orbán into something more influential than the actual role he probably plays in a large and fragmented European alliance.

Orbán also aims to showcase himself as leader of a "new EU," one that he hopes would replace the current dysfunctional behemoth. He frequently posts friendly images with the European right wing—a representative example is his almost flirting photographs with Giorgia Meloni, who is currently the prime minister of Italy. Meloni is famous for her anti-LGBTQ stance in the European Union, in particular her firm opposition to gay marriage and gay civil unions. The first image shows an outsized Orbán, in a very traditional male role, yet in an informal setting (fig. 3.7). The second image steps up the game of flirtation, emphasized by the caption in Italian: AVANTI RAGAZZA! (fig. 3.8).

Orbán Viktor ✔
28 August 2021 · 🌐

···

Due fratelli. Találkozó Giorgia Melonival. ≈▮▮

👍 45K   2.3K comments   713 shares

FIG. 3.7. "Due fratelli. Meeting with Giorgia Meloni." Posted by Viktor Orbán on Facebook, August 28, 2021.

This kind of friendly imagery with illiberal leaders also extends beyond the boundaries of the European Union. A characteristic example was Orbán's bonding with Brazilian president Bolsonaro (fig. 3.9). On yet another Facebook photograph, he was beaming with pride as he was speaking

Orbán Viktor ✓
14 September at 10:03 · 🌐

Isten hozta Giorgia Melonit, Olaszország miniszterelnökét!

AVANTI RAGAZZA!

❬Ⅴ❭ **Orbán Viktor**

👍 3.7K   439 comments 117 shares

FIG. 3.8. "Welcome Giorgia Meloni, Prime Minister of Italy!" / "Avanti Ragazza!" Posted by Viktor Orbán on Facebook, September 14, 2023.

to former US president Trump on the phone (fig. 3.10). This photographic rendering of international illiberal alliances signals Orbán's ambition to appear as a globally significant player in a postliberal world.

A particularly powerful example of visualizing illiberal networks was a post when Orbán decided to put on the red

Orbán Viktor ✔ · Follow
February 17, 2022 · 🌐

Minden olyan törekvés, amely a béke megőrzését segíti, Magyarország érdekeivel egyezik.

See Translation

Brazília elnöke
Magyarországon

Orbán Viktor

👍 10K   1.7K comments   825 shares

👍 Like   💬 Comment   ↪ Share

FIG. 3.9. "Every effort that aims at preserving peace aligns with Hungary's interests." Posted by Viktor Orbán on Facebook, February 17, 2022.

Orbán Viktor ✔ · Follow
January 18, 2022 · 🌐

Telefonos egyeztetés Donald Trump korábbi amerikai elnökkel

See Translation

A vonalban:
Donald Trump

Orbán Viktor

👍😂 41K   5.6K comments   1K shares

👍 Like   ○ Comment   ↪ Share

FIG. 3.10. "Phone negotiation with former American President Donald Trump." / "On the line: Donald Trump." Posted by Viktor Orbán on Facebook, January 18, 2022.

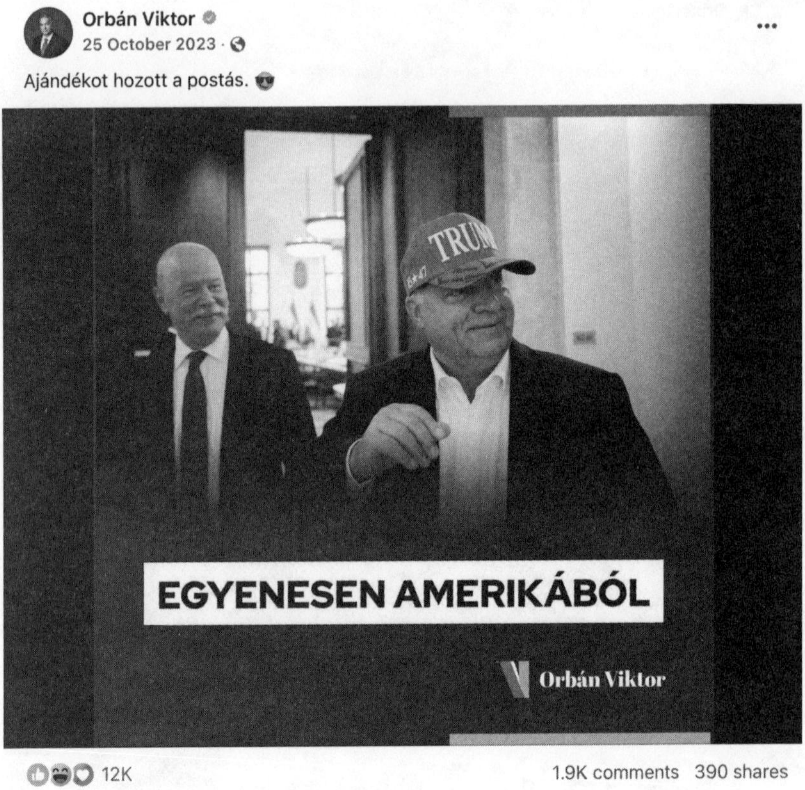

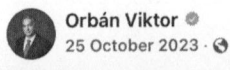

Orbán Viktor ✓
25 October 2023 · ⊙

Ajándékot hozott a postás. 🐢

EGYENESEN AMERIKÁBÓL

〡 Orbán Viktor

👍😄❤ 12K   1.9K comments   390 shares

FIG. 3.11. "The mailman brought a gift." / "Straight from the United
States." Posted by Viktor Orbán on Facebook, October 25, 2023.

MAGA hat, the iconic object of former president Trump and
a key visual marker of Trump's reelection campaign in 2024
(fig. 3.11). In this case Orbán was physically fusing with the
MAGA movement. The posted image on Facebook donned
a headline: "Straight from the United States," while the
related caption proudly announced: "The mailman brought
a gift. 🐢" Words seem no longer enough to express connection; physical touch and corporeal fusion becomes a must.

Charismatic Dominance as Authenticity Performance

Finally, a regular characteristic of Orbán's image is his relentless, lonely, and heroic fight against a wide variety of enemies. This fighter image is closer to a traditional form of charisma (building on distance from audiences) than to contemporary approaches of charm (building on proximity to audiences). Given Orbán's now more than three decades of activity in Hungarian professional politics, it is challenging for him to appear as a charming newcomer or an outsider. He is part of the elite and has been for a long time. Still, through identifying some stronger elites outside of the country, he can still appear as a new "superhero" on the global stage. In the case of international alliances, Orbán also makes sure he appears as an important player in these organizations, whose voice matters in global politics.

Orbán portrays his tribe as a homogenous group, respecting tradition, Christianity, whiteness, and the nation, and he presents his people in opposition to modern, secular, diverse, and international communities. In his view several enemies threaten his tribe: former prime minister Ferenc Gyurcsány; American financier and philanthropist George Soros and his son, Alexander Soros; American president Biden; the American Democrats; Brussels; Ukrainian president Zelensky; the gender lobby; and migrants, among others. All these adversaries have a common goal: destroying the nation by forcing it to accept values that are incompatible with Hungarian traditions as defined by Orbán.

Orbán's protective narratives rely on direct references to the will of the people, the construction of a moral majority, and the promise of a powerful and protective state. His central narrative revolves around three frequently repeated tropes: referring to himself as David from the Old Testament in his fight against Goliath (the West in general and the European Union in particular); a differentiation between "we" (the Fidesz community) and "they" (for instance George Soros and Ferenc Gyurcsány); and a persistent comedic, bullying representation of the Hungarian oppositional leaders and parties. These central narratives and imaginaries are also in conflict with each other. On the one hand Orbán presents himself as the small and vulnerable David in an existential fight against Goliath in Brussels. He sometimes extends this image to the whole of his community of voters, referring to "Davids" in plural. For instance, in a characteristic image, he walks with a group of supporters on Liberty Bridge in Budapest—a symbolic site to present an existential fight against the West (fig. 3.12). The supporters wear Hungarian folk costumes, underlining the message of respectable Hungarian tradition versus arrogant foreign interference.

At the same time, while making fun of the opposition, Orbán often takes on the role of the bully. In one image, Orbán and Fidesz MPs laugh at one of the key figures of the opposition, the leader of the oppositional party Jobbik (fig. 3.13).[21] To bring some coherence to his image, Orbán mostly keeps the David references for international fights and his strong bully image for domestic politics—although not exclusively, as he also occasionally presents himself as a hacker and a fighter in international debates.

Orbán enacts a specifically masculine charisma in his response to the international movement of athletes who kneel at the beginning of sports games—a political performance started by former NFL quarterback Colin Kaepernick in 2016 against racial injustice in the United States. Orbán is against

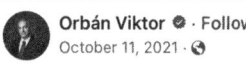

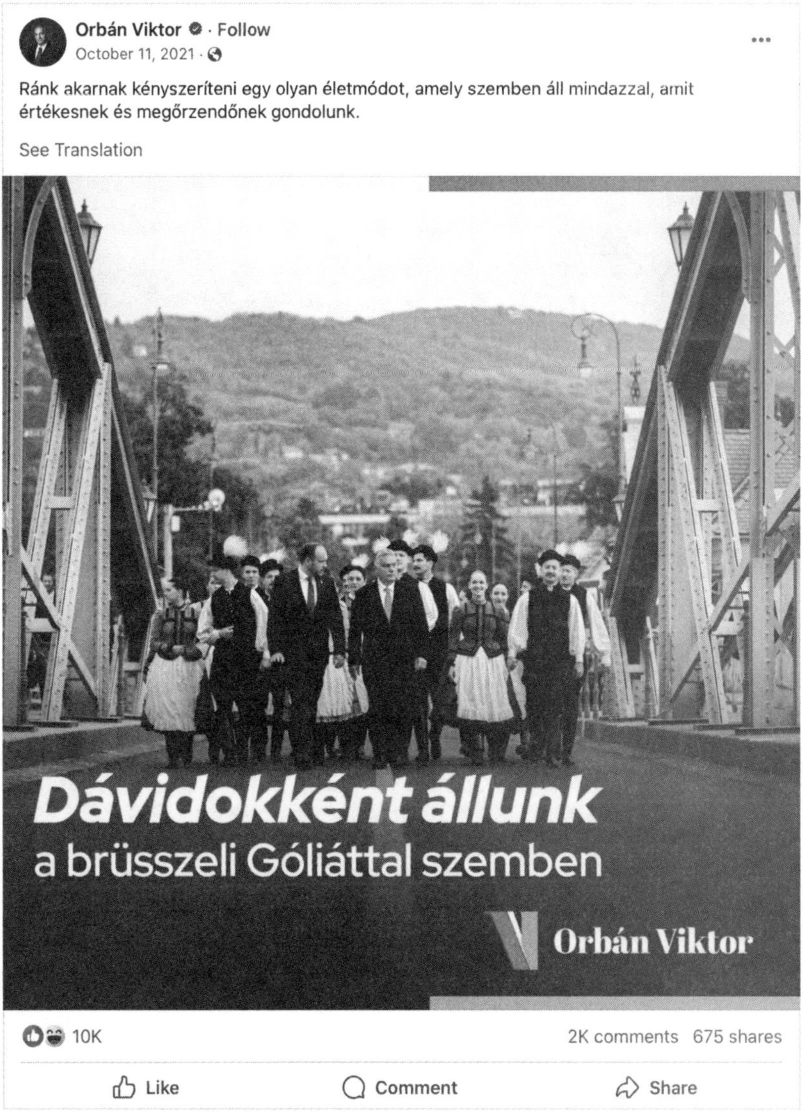
Orbán Viktor · Follow
October 11, 2021 ·
Ránk akarnak kényszeríteni egy olyan életmódot, amely szemben áll mindazzal, amit értékesnek és megőrzendőnek gondolunk.
See Translation
Dávidokként állunk
a brüsszeli Góliáttal szemben
Orbán Viktor
10K
2K comments 675 shares
Like
Comment
Share

FIG. 3.12. “They want to force us into a lifestyle that is the opposite of everything we regard as valuable and worthy of protection.” / “We stand as Davids against the Goliath of Brussels.” Posted by Viktor Orbán on Facebook, October 11, 2021.

Orbán Viktor ✔ · Follow
September 20, 2021 · 🌐

A Gyurcsány-show folytatódik.
A bohóc szerepében: Jakab Péter. 🃏

See Translation

A GYURCSÁNY-SHOW FOLYTATÓDIK.

A bohóc szerepében: JAKAB PÉTER.

Orbán Viktor

👍😆 10K   5.8K comments 1.2K shares

FIG. 3.13. "The Gyurcsány-show continues. In the role of the clown: Péter Jakab." Posted by Viktor Orbán on Facebook, September 20, 2021.

this practice, arguing that Hungarians kneel only in three cases: in front of God, in front of their home country, and in the moment of proposing to their beloved. "Any other case is against our cultural traditions," he argued in a Facebook video.[22] Orbán emphasized that Hungarian soccer players "should win, and if they cannot, they should die while still standing." While in the context of sports, this video encapsulated both Orbán's understanding of masculinity as a persistent fight and his personal aversion to the popular political protest performance that has gained traction worldwide with the Black Lives Matter movement.

In anticipation of the upcoming elections in 2022, the dominance theme was more focused on creating a coherent domestic voter community. The militaristic references were used to mobilize in the name of the nation. A series of photographs showed Orbán as speaking to admiring crowds of Hungarian soldiers or regular voters. Typical headlines included "Together We Are the Power" and "For the Homeland." Orbán also often presented himself as the defender of Christianity, fighting to save the heritage of "Christian Europe." With his evocation of Christianity, Orbán sacralized the public sphere and legitimized his actions through nonrational means.

In 2022, the Hungarian prime minister had to face an actual war right at the borders of his country: Russia's invasion of Ukraine starting on February 24, 2022. After an initial phase of relative confusion, Orbán firmly articulated his response: the need to exhibit an attitude of what he termed "strategic calmness." In a rather distanced tone, he advocated for defending Hungarian interests in the conflict. In a swift move, he dropped the "fighter" image and assumed the role of a calm, mature politician. In addition to frequent Facebook posts communicating this message of strategic calmness, government posters were placed all around the country, emphasizing the need to protect Hungary (not Ukraine). In his communication about the war, Orbán emerged as both a charismatic, faraway leader and a gentle protector of the Hungarian nation. His gray-haired, wise-man images supported this message (fig. 3.14). Related texts argued that he was ready to protect Hungary in times of war. His wartime communication did not include any references to 1956, the year when Hungary was invaded by the Soviet Union and desperately looked for international support as tens of thousands of Hungarian refugees were fleeing the country.

Concluding Thoughts on Illiberal Charm

Orbán's Facebook profile presents him as both a charming (proximate) and a charismatic (distanced) leader who assumes the role of the nation's symbolic condensation. He is shown as an authentic leader who is morally and ideologically one with the community whose boundaries he draws. His iconic representations embody the core messages he aims to communicate: ethnic homogeneity, Christianity, tradition, and "Hungary first." While analysts often talk about his powerful capture of the media landscape, he also masterfully captures hearts through his illiberal charm and concentrated messaging across a wide variety of platforms.

When looking at Orbán's charm on social media, some of the international analyses of him that speak of an "aggressive fascist leader" seem two-dimensional. His constructed online persona is multilayered, ranging from aggressor to animal lover, and ever shifting, from fighter in peaceful times to an advocate of "strategic calmness" in an actual war.

FIG. 3.14. "Let's preserve Hungary's peace and security!" Government poster in Budapest, photo taken by Julia Sonnevend, March 2022.

Orbán occasionally also exhibits more traditionally charismatic qualities, for instance in his speeches at rallies and in his weekly radio interviews. The building blocks of this image are constantly being adapted to the current political situation based on regularly conducted public opinion polls, with easy-to-understand messages that are optimized for Hungarian society and Fidesz's political interests. The Orbán image lacks definite principles, but its popularity remains steadfast despite the contradictions. Facts do not counter the myth and the cult he has built up, as Orbán's popularity ultimately rests on his charm and on the belief that he personally embodies the nation.

The performative power of populism builds on the followers' belief that the body of the populist leader represents their own identity, "concretely and physically."[23] For the political leader's charismatic and charming characteristics to resonate with audiences, he needs to become something of an icon of the values he wants to communicate. Icons work as symbolic condensations. As American sociologist Jeffrey C. Alexander put it, "they root generic, social meanings in a specific and 'material' form."[24] The image of the populist leader comes to stand for the broad set of values he aims to communicate. The political leader cannot fully represent the nation, but he comes to stand for it, just as iconic photographs cannot represent events fully, yet they come to stand for them. The iconic leader draws the boundaries of the nation, ultimately deciding who belongs and who does not.

Viktor Orbán has become one of the icons of right-wing identity and a node in the global network of right-wing movements. Orbán's image ultimately rests on a myth,[25] presenting a powerful story of heroes and villains. The world is divided between "us" and "them," and every interaction with "them" is a fight. Protecting and threatening narratives thus emerge, and they are easy to comprehend and apply. In the center of the myth stands the authentic, charismatic, and charming hero, who attacks or defends depending on the tribe's needs. The hero is untouchable through rational arguments or facts. The power of his personality rules above all.

Jacinda Ardern (the liberal icon) and Viktor Orbán (the illiberal icon) could not be more different when it comes to their political messaging. Yet, in both cases we see a dramatic breakthrough of personality to connect with constituencies. In addition to fusion with their local tribes, they also achieved an outsized image on the global stage in the form of a hero or a villain, depending on the viewer's political stance.

In Ardern's and Orbán's communication, charm was a persistent feature, used almost every step of the way. But constructing charm is not always a long-term process with the aim to build lasting public personas. Charm can also be deployed short term to swiftly shift public perceptions about a particular issue. The next two chapters will focus on charm offensives, when charm is briefly weaponized for an immediate political goal.

4

Charm Offensive in Diplomacy

IRANIAN FOREIGN MINISTER MOHAMMAD JAVAD ZARIF

In early 2015, at the height of the American-Iranian nuclear deal negotiations, Iran's foreign minister, Mohammad Javad Zarif, took a short walk with then US secretary of state John Kerry in Geneva. They were deeply immersed in their conversation, gesturing in a trusting, almost friendly manner (fig. 4.1). The images rocked social media worldwide. Zarif was immediately under fire in Iran for such a public show of proximity with the United States. A petition published in the hard-line *Fars News* argued that "given the Great Satan's endless demands and sabotage during the course of the nuclear negotiations, there is no conceivable ground for intimacy between the foreign ministers of Iran and America."[1] Western journalists, meanwhile, increasingly looked at Iran as a country that can attract readers' interest through a relatable and charming personality.

FIG. 4.1. US secretary of state John Kerry (*right*), speaks with Iranian foreign minister Mohammad Javad Zarif (*left*), as they walk in the city of Geneva, Switzerland, January 14, 2015, during a bilateral meeting ahead of the next round of nuclear discussions, which begin on January 15. EPA.

While often neglected in international relations research, personal qualities and connections strongly matter in diplomacy.[2] Countries often employ strategic public relations campaigns to shift their international image through their leaders' personal magnetism. A negative country image can cripple a leader's ability to shape foreign relations, make relevant deals, and rally the international community for causes. In these cases, a charm offensive can come to the rescue. Charm offensives project mediated friendliness with the help of smiles, embraces, friendly walks, and other visible signs of geniality or warmth in public diplomatic settings.

Leaders perform these amicable acts for international audiences. The global media then extensively cover these performances on a variety of platforms, helping a country go through a swift, and often temporary, image makeover.

Mohammad Javad Zarif sustained his charm offensive throughout the American-Iranian nuclear deal negotiations, creating a space of communication where signing the deal became a possibility. Looking at his charm offensives' American and Israeli press coverage, this chapter highlights that even in the most rational context, the tedious negotiations of a nuclear deal, nonrational factors like charm and personal appeal play a crucial role in diplomacy.

Iran's nuclear program began in the late 1950s under the shah's regime, which declared that its purpose was to provide electricity to a modernizing country. After the Islamic Revolution in 1979, Iran continued to pursue its nuclear program, arguing that the program had only a peaceful purpose. Many in the international community became suspicious of Iran's intentions, questioning the peaceful purpose of the country's nuclear program, and reminding observers that Iran had hidden nuclear facilities and breached international agreements before. Economic sanctions against Iran intensified under the rule of the hard-liner president Mahmoud Ahmadinejad (2005–13) and led to the country's international isolation and a severe economic crisis.[3]

In early August 2013 the election of Hassan Rouhani to the presidency and the appointment of Mohammad Javad Zarif as foreign minister marked a change in Iran's willingness to negotiate its nuclear program. In 2015 the two superpowers engaged in extensive negotiations to reach a final deal. Many critics in the West viewed these negotiations with suspicion; Iran's ongoing intervention in civil wars in Syria and Yemen particularly triggered questions. Iran desperately needed a quick image makeover in Western media to make a future nuclear deal possible.

Zarif was the ideal politician to lead Iran's charm offensive given his fluency in English language and American culture. He moved to the United States as a teenager and later completed his PhD at the University of Denver in international relations. He eventually became a senior member of the Iranian foreign service, serving as the Iranian ambassador to the United Nations. A policy paper Zarif published in the prestigious journal *Foreign Affairs* reflected the new spirit Zarif brought to Iranian diplomacy. In his analysis, Zarif diverged from Iran's former adversarial foreign policy and stated that Iran was seeking to "foster peace and security at the regional and international levels through positive engagement."[4] This message of positive engagement became the central message of Iran's and Zarif's charm offensive.

The month of March 2015, the focus of this chapter, was crucial as the Iranian and American teams were trying to finalize the deal in an extensive series of talks, which took place mainly in Lausanne, Switzerland. But the drama was performed on other stages as well during this month. Simultaneously, conservative US representatives did not agree with the Obama administration's foreign policy and sought to undermine it with the 2016 elections on the horizon. Iranian hard-liners opposed any concessions on the nuclear program and were unhappy with the intimate relations forged between the Iranian and American negotiating teams. Israeli prime minister Benjamin Netanyahu wanted to make sure the international community would not revoke the sanction regime against Iran as he was among the sanctions' proud architects. Speaker of the House John Boehner invited Netanyahu to speak to the Congress without coordinating the visit with President Obama. Netanyahu flew to Washington and delivered a dramatic speech against the deal on March 3, 2015. In his speech, Netanyahu emphasized the dangers Zarif's seductive techniques posed; he even used the term "charm" explicitly: "the same Zarif who charms Western diplomats laid a wreath at the grave of Imad Mughniyeh. Imad Mughniyeh is the terrorist mastermind who spilled more American blood than any other terrorist besides Osama bin Laden. I'd like to see someone ask him a question about that."[5]

As Netanyahu's speech showed, "charm" was a key trope of hope or concern during the negotiations, depending on whose perspective you take. The debate highlighted charm's duality as a force of both seduction and deception. Through the analysis of coverage of Zarif's charm offensive in the American and Israeli press during the fateful month of March 2015, we can see how Zarif weaponized charm for an important cause, and also how Western journalists interpreted and presented his actions.

Fusion through Normalization and Partnership

The press's focus was on the process of calm negotiation, not on explosive events. The "process" had become the new normal, including mundane news coverage of it. Audiences who were used to reading about Iran in the context of exceptional events like war and terror now heard about it on a daily basis, as Iran was framed as a partner state, led by a relatable foreign minister with whom the United States can strike a deal. There was not a single day throughout March 2015 without reports about this topic in the US mainstream press. In this sense, negotiations were not only means; they were also an end. The aim of the charm offensive was to reframe and routinize Iran as a legitimate partner.

This normalization was badly needed. Iran was amid various divisive interventions across the Middle East in 2015. Political leaders in Saudi Arabia, with whom Iran had a very strained relationship, strongly opposed the nuclear deal. For the success of Iran's charm offensive it was crucial to avoid discussing Iran's conflicts not only in the past but also in the present. For instance, when asked in an interview about Iran's "support for terror," Zarif avoided giving a clear answer.[6] When this avoidance technique was not sufficient, the Iranian leadership tried to shift the conversation so it would emphasize problems in American diplomacy. For example, Ayatollah Ali Khamenei wrote a response letter to the American senators who opposed the deal, stating that "some think that the United States does not need to act cunningly or do tricks . . . but the Americans need to use tricks and deception a lot, and they are doing the same now, and this reality worries us."[7] By launching this attack, Khamenei managed to flip the American argument on its head, arguing that the United States, not Iran, is the country that could not be trusted. While using more restrained language than Khamenei, Zarif reflected a similar skepticism toward American trustworthiness.[8]

Many were concerned that with the message of "calm negotiation," Iran might be intentionally prolonging the process. For instance, the head of the International Atomic Energy Agency argued that Iran was trying to buy time by turning the negotiations into an "endless process." He complained that progress had been very limited in the agency's interaction with Iran, adding that the country addressed only one issue out of a twelve-step work plan it had agreed on with the agency.[9] But despite these moments of criticism, the extended process of negotiation along with steady, calm, and detailed press coverage in the United States presented a normalized image of Iran as a reliable actor in international diplomacy.

Zarif also attempted to fuse with his audience by framing the negotiations in Switzerland as a form of partnership. He tried to solidify the negotiations as legitimate for both the international community and his domestic critics. Zarif thus framed the nuclear deal as being about the "dignity" of the involved nations. This stance is particularly important historically, given that Iran's partners were Western powers, the former colonizers. Zarif used the social media platform Twitter to spread the message that Iranians had already made their choice, and they chose "engagement with dignity"; therefore it was "high time for the U.S. and its allies to choose: pressure or agreement."[10] Zarif argued that economic sanctions were a form of humiliation and had to be lifted altogether. Insisting that Iran's nuclear program was solely designed for civilian, peaceful purposes such as generating electricity, Zarif refused to accept the "excessive demand" of the Obama administration to freeze the Iranian nuclear program for ten years.[11]

It was not only Zarif who emphasized the notion of dignity, partnership, and flattened hierarchy to achieve fusion. American news outlets put considerable efforts into portraying Zarif as a relatable partner in negotiation. For instance, the *New York Times* emphasized those contextual details about the Iranian foreign minister that would sound familiar and trustworthy to the American audience: "On Sunday, Secretary of State John Kerry flew to Switzerland to meet again with Mohammad Javad Zarif, the Iranian Foreign

Minister who earned a PhD in international law and policy from the University of Denver."[12] The portrayal of similarities between Iranian and American diplomats came to its peak in another *New York Times* story about the technical experts of both teams. The story revealed that both the American Ernest J. Moniz and the Iranian Ali Akbar Salehi went to MIT, and they had a similar life trajectory: "at the Massachusetts Institute of Technology in the mid-1970s, Ernest J. Moniz was an up-and-coming nuclear scientist in search of tenure, and Ali Akbar Salehi, a brilliant Iranian graduate student, was finishing a dissertation on fast-neutron reactors. The two did not know each other, but they followed similar paths once they left the campus."[13] In this case, American journalists took the initiative to emphasize similarities between the negotiating partners, even though Moniz and Salehi had never actually met at MIT.

Zarif's charm offensive also aimed to achieve fusion with the audience by focusing on a shared, positive future. By emphasizing shared destiny and mutual interest, he created the possibility for his international audience to momentarily come together over the issue of the nuclear deal. Zarif frequently pointed out that a successful nuclear agreement, based on mutual respect, could create a better world for everyone. The conditions for creating this world had to be met in the immediate future, as Iran rejected a scenario in which sanctions would be lifted through a slow step-by-step process.[14] Zarif also tried to put the Iranian nuclear deal in a global perspective focusing on a shared global future, promoting a hopeful message. Inspired by the Iranian holiday Nowruz and Secretary Kerry's related greetings, Zarif said on March 20: "I hope this new day will be a new day for the entire world."[15]

The flattened hierarchy between Zarif and his Western counterparts was apparent not only in texts, but also in news photographs. In the vast majority of press photos in which Zarif appeared with another person he was presented as that person's equal. This means that both Zarif and the other person were shown "at the same level," either sitting or standing on the same platform. In one photograph, the European Union's foreign policy chief, Federica Mogherini, and Zarif are standing next to each other with their respective flags in the background (fig. 4.2). They also use similar body language, with both hands held close to their bodies.

A deeper connection between Zarif and his American counterparts appeared in a photo taken right before Zarif's meeting with Kerry (fig. 4.3). Both were standing in the center, accompanied by their technical experts—the American Moniz and the Iranian Salehi looked relaxed and comfortable. The respective national flags in the background completed a symmetrical image. The photograph communicated a deep connection forged between Zarif and Kerry that went beyond regular diplomatic relations. Almost touching arms, they looked intently into each other's eyes. Zarif even displayed a warm smile. The image radiated connection, almost friendship, well beyond diplomatic expectations.

Demasking through Persistent Interactions and "Smile Offensives"

In almost all Western photos analyzed, Zarif was in the company of other people, either Western diplomats or other members of the Iranian team in Lausanne. By showing Zarif in interaction, the process of negotiations was underscored. In comparison, Israeli prime minister Benjamin Netanyahu's

FIG. 4.2. European Union foreign policy chief Federica Mogherini poses with Iranian foreign minister Mohammad Javad Zarif (*left*) ahead of nuclear talks in Brussels, March 16, 2015. REUTERS / Francois Lenoir.

FIG. 4.3. US energy secretary Ernest Moniz, US secretary of state John Kerry, Iran's foreign minister Mohammad Javad Zarif and head of the Atomic Energy Organization of Iran Ali Akbar Salehi (*left to right*) pose for a photograph before resuming talks over Iran's nuclear program in Lausanne, March 16, 2015. REUTERS / Brian Snyder.

representation was dramatically different during the same period by the exact same news outlets. A third of Netanyahu's Western press photos from March 2015 showed the Israeli prime minister by himself. This "loneliness" in imagery signaled, whether intended or not, that his position was not supported by many.

Western journalists described Zarif as a serious diplomat who came to Lausanne with a genuine intention to improve the relationship between Iran and the West, forging meaningful partnerships. Photographs that showed him with other Iranian diplomats were particularly illustrative of this point. For instance, in a news image Zarif was depicted as having a lively argument with his technical expert Salehi, while other members of the Iranian team listened to him carefully. Zarif appeared as a good listener, a quality that could help fuse with both his negotiation partners and his global audience. Many of the news photographs showed press conferences or came from official press releases. Their message of friendly relations was preplanned, as Zarif and other negotiators anticipated being photographed in official diplomatic settings. They shook hands and joined friendly walks knowing their charm offensive would attract international media attention.

The flattened hierarchy and partnership Zarif tried to construct between Iran and the West was also visible in his persistent smiles in press photographs. Zarif's enchanting smiles did not go unnoticed by the international media. The Israeli press coined the term "smile offensive" to describe Zarif's warm diplomatic strategy.[16] Zarif himself spoke about his use of smiles in diplomatic negotiations, stating in his 2013 memoir that "you should always smile in diplomacy, but you should never forget you are talking to an enemy."[17] His warm smiles throughout the nuclear negotiations made him relatable and a popular subject to display on the front pages of Western news outlets.

Restaging: Controlled Settings

Zarif's charm offensive preferred calm negotiations behind closed doors, with only occasional media spectacles. He focused on forging close personal relationships with his Western colleagues, especially with Kerry. This delicate process of endearment mostly took place far away from the media. The closed-door strategy led to media coverage containing very little factual or contextual information on the negotiations. For instance, the Israeli *Haaretz* only mentioned that "the American foreign minister John Kerry and his Iranian colleague, Mohammad Javad Zarif, met yesterday in the city of Lausanne in Switzerland for five hours to discuss the Iranian nuclear program."[18] These private interactions did not stop with the leaders of the negotiating teams. They trickled down to the technical experts. American journalists noted that the American Ernest Moniz and the Iranian Ali Akbar Salehi also "dropped formality" and disappeared for hours at a time into the conference room at the hotel in Lausanne.[19]

While the long, closed-door meetings between the negotiating counterparts seemed routine and mundane from a Western perspective, they were very problematic for some Iranian hard-liners. Mohammad Reza Naghi, head commander of the powerful paramilitary organization Basij, said that the friendly interactions of Zarif and Kerry were "a show of intimacy with the enemy of humanity." Yet, according to a *New York Times* rendering of the events, after Zarif explained to Ayatollah Khamenei that refusing interactions like the afternoon stroll "would have been a diplomatic faux pas, the leader agreed and all criticism ended."[20] This example shows that Zarif's intimate use of his charm came at a great personal and political risk. But overall, Zarif was able to control the settings where key interactions took place. He strategically and carefully avoided unpredictable events where hostilities could erupt. He masterfully navigated an array of stages for his charm offensive, from well-photographed friendly walks to closed-door negotiations (a hidden stage) with the aim to reach tangible results in the historic nuclear negotiations with the United States.

Concluding Thoughts

There were four major characteristics of Zarif's charm offensive: a focus on future ramifications; a desire to limit the scope of the interaction to mundane negotiations; a flattened hierarchy; and mostly closed-door settings. Western journalists enthusiastically covered these "unexpected" features of the Iranian diplomacy and ultimately helped Zarif achieve a favorable international media environment conducive to reaching an international agreement. Many journalists presented Zarif as a negotiator who focused on the future, the process, the mundane, and friendly interactions, facilitating a reciprocal partnership between the American and Iranian teams. They portrayed Zarif, both in texts and in photographs, as a new type of charming Iranian leader who, through his warm gestures, offered a peaceful vision for the Middle East.

Zarif's charm offensive was inherently performative. It was intended not just for the immediate negotiation partners, but for a broad international audience that was watching the negotiations unfold between Iran and the West. Zarif walked with Secretary Kerry along the banks of Lake Geneva despite harsh criticism at home because he needed to manufacture intimacy with the American leader. His charm offensive was a form of mediated friendliness designed to transform the public image of the country he represented. It was a concentrated effort synchronized between news outlets and politicians for a limited amount of time to achieve a clear political goal. Zarif focused on the future in contrast to the confusing past; he aimed at a calm and narrowly defined process of negotiations and preferred closed-door discussions among experts and one-on-one conversations with

Secretary of State Kerry over public press conferences. He warmly welcomed photographers with smiles and presented a persistent readiness for friendly interaction. Western journalists welcomed these moments to present the confusing, faraway happenings of the nuclear deal negotiations in a relatable way.

Successful social performances depend on the ability to communicate one's performances as true and authentic expressions.[21] Whether Zarif convinced his audiences about true intentions or not, his charm offensive could very well be described as effective, creating a relatable and welcoming setting for the nuclear deal's signing. The agreement was eventually signed on July 14, 2015, in Vienna. The signatories were the five permanent members of the United Nations Security Council (China, France, Russia, the United Kingdom, and the United States) plus Germany and the European Union. The "Iranian nuclear deal" was presented as a major event, a historic diplomatic achievement that meant to ensure the peaceful nature of Iran's nuclear program.

At the same time, Zarif's charm offensive's long-term effects are more disputable. In May 2018, President Trump withdrew the United States from the Iranian nuclear deal, which he perceived as a key foreign policy mistake of the Obama administration. Relations between Iran and the United States remain very tense to this day, calling into question the legacy of the 2015 negotiations. The conflictual relations between Iran and the United States regularly cause intense worry in the international community that a military conflict might be erupting in the foreseeable future. The arrival of the Biden administration softened these worries somewhat, since Biden was vice president during the nuclear deal negotiations, but did not erase them. In 2022, the State Department issued multiple statements of condemnation against Iran. On November 3, 2022, President Biden vowed to "free Iran" and expressed his support for the ongoing protests in the country. As of the writing of this chapter, the resuscitation of the Iranian nuclear deal seems an extremely distant possibility. Zarif's charm offensive, while spectacular at its time, seems to be ephemeral in the long run. As the world is directing its attention toward more recent charm offensives on the global stage, Zarif's maneuvers, while impressive, increasingly fade in memory.

5

Unexpected Charm

NORTH KOREAN LEADER KIM JONG-UN

In the summer of 2018 Kim Jong-un shocked the world: he took a selfie. An image of Kim and the Singapore ministers of foreign affairs and education went viral on Twitter (fig. 5.1). The effort was part of a larger effort to change the leader's somewhat frightening global image. The *New York Times* coverage underlined journalists' surprise, as one article put it: "Before the meeting, Mr. Kim posed for a selfie with Singapore's foreign minister, as if he were a fraternity brother blowing off his senior thesis for a night on the town."[1] In an unexpected twist of personality, Kim was actively exploiting the features of digital media.

With a swift charm offensive over six months in 2018, Kim Jong-un radically changed his image on the global stage, at least temporarily. First, Kim's New Year's Day address proposed increased collaboration with South Korea to create a

Vivian Balakrishnan ✓
@VivianBala

···

#Jalanjalan #guesswhwere?

9:42 AM · Jun 11, 2018

FIG. 5.1. "#Jalanjalan #guesswhwere?" Posted by Vivian Balakrishnan, Singapore minister of foreign affairs, on Twitter, June 11, 2018.

peaceful environment on the Korean Peninsula. Then in a quick procession of events, in February 2018 North Korea participated in the Winter Olympics; in April the inter-Korea summit was held for the first time in eleven years; and June marked the first meeting of a US president and a North Korean leader ever in history. During these six months, in President Trump's communications Kim was miraculously transformed from a "little rocket man" to an "honorable" leader.[2] How did this radical metamorphosis happen?

Since Kim Il-sung founded the Democratic People's Republic of North Korea (DPRK) in 1948, the Kim family has ruled North Korea—Kim Il-sung until his death in 1994, then his son, Kim Jong-il, until his death in 2011, and now grandson, Kim Jong-un. Throughout its history, North Korea has been known to oscillate between friendly gestures and offensive military threats, especially in relation to South Korea.[3] Examples of peaceful communication during the Kim Il-sung and Kim Jong-il regimes include North-South family reunion events, participating in six-party talks, opening Mount Kumgang to tourists, taking part in the Busan Asian Games, and South and North Korean athletes marching together at the opening ceremony of the Sydney Olympic Games.[4] At the same time, there were limited opportunities for actual dialogue between North and South Korea during the Kim Il-sung era because North Korea mostly performed coercive diplomacy through armed provocation.[5] Propagating self-reliance ideology as a central feature of his regime, Kim Il-sung maintained a hostile relationship with the United States.[6] Although his son, Kim Jong-il, seemed to seek change in foreign policy to overcome North Korea's economic hardship,[7] the Kim Jong-il regime still mainly sought military solutions when dealing with diplomatic issues.[8] Constructing their respective images as authoritative military leaders, both Kim Il-sung and Kim Jong-il rarely made international appearances and were regularly described as reclusive dictators.[9] For a brief period in 2018, Kim Jong-un broke with this style of the past.

Authenticity Performance—Kim Jong-un's Increasing Openness to News Photography

Casting away North Korea's image as a "hermit kingdom," Kim Jong-un increasingly opened up to the media to show his leadership to the wider world. Unlike his predecessors, who mostly kept their diplomatic practices behind the scenes, Kim actively invited the media's attention and appeared on the global stage whenever possible. The April 2018 inter-Korean summit was broadcast live across the world.[10] Confidential negotiations between Kim Jong-un and South Korean president Moon Jae-in were visually disclosed as the two leaders engaged in one-on-one conversation during a walk. Kim even appeared in front of tourists and citizens the night before the Trump-Kim summit, waving to the cameras.[11] As journalists captured Kim's every move, his human characteristics were unveiled. The whole world was watching.

Kim Jong-un did not merely appear in front of the cameras; he also took the initiative to actively shape North Korea's media coverage. Most notably, he sent his youngest sister, Kim Yo-jong, to the PyeongChang Winter Olympics. She was the first person in the Kim family to set foot on South Korean soil since the Korean War. The unprecedented nature of her visit and the public's curiosity over Kim Jong-un's relatively unknown sister led international media to follow her closely. The *New York Times* commented that Kim Yo-jong created a "media frenzy,"[12] while the *Wall Street Journal* called this phenomenon "media's dictatorship indulgence."[13] The *Washington Post* mentioned that she was "the object of most South Korean fascination," observing that Kim Yo-jong was "surrounded by the kind of paparazzi throng and security detail that are usually the preserve of K-pop Stars."[14]

Kim Jong-un's sister was portrayed as a winner of a "charm competition,"[15] as she attracted more media attention than then American vice president Mike Pence during the Winter Olympics. News articles emphasized that she was "taking Pence's spotlight," "outflank[ed] Trump's envoy,"[16] and "stole much of the show."[17] South Korean media also spoke in a similar vein, presenting Ivanka Trump's visit to the Olympics as a "PR game with Kim Yo-jong"[18] and acknowledging that Kim Yo-jong could even "win a gold medal for her diplomatic maneuvers."[19]

Frequently using words such as "pageantry" and "spectacle" when describing North Korea's recent media performances, both American and South Korean journalists understood North Korea's diplomatic strategies to be heavily concentrated on visual appearance and spectacle. Media representations of North Korea's charm offensive zoomed in on minor visual details, such as Kim Jong-un's stylistic change. Journalists highlighted the leader's American makeover, from his adoption of a Western hairstyle and suit to his decision to outfit North Korean cheerleaders in Nike baseball caps during the PyeongChang Winter Olympics.[20]

Restaging—Planned Image Campaigns and Improvisation in New Settings

Both American and South Korean media depicted Kim Jong-un's shift in international diplomacy as a deliberate public relations strategy.[21] For example, the *New York Times* assessed North Korea's diplomatic overture during the early months of 2018 as something that was "planned methodically"[22] and "plotted for months."[23] Similarly, the South Korean *Hankyoreh* commented that North Korea's "changes in international diplomacy were under Kim Jong-un's detailed roadmap,"[24] explaining that Kim's recent diplomatic overture was far from spontaneous.

Kim's performance during international media events, such as the inter-Korean summits and the Trump-Kim summit, was also described as extensively rehearsed showmanship. An opinion piece from a leading South Korean newspaper on the inter-Korean summit reflected this sentiment: "Every scene of the summit was meticulously planned and played by the script that was written to move the audience and maximize the dramatic effect of Kim's performance."[25] American media spoke in a similar vein when reporting the Trump-Kim summit, portraying Kim's actions as "expertly choreographed, sophisticated stagecraft."[26] Journalists were careful not to take North Korea's softened diplomatic gestures at face value; they rather attempted to scrutinize North Korea's underlying motives.

Yet, Kim Jong-un's performance did not only consist of highly planned events. He also wanted to send the message that he was capable of improvising—although perhaps these were also highly planned "improvisations." A key example was Kim's crossing the demilitarized zone while holding hands with South Korean president Moon (fig. 5.2). Covering this unexpected, live broadcast performance, the South Korean *Chosun* wrote that such "impromptu allowed Kim to show his flexibility and openness, as well as the sincerity of his recent diplomatic transformations."[27] The *New York Times* also mentioned that this encounter "transfixed television viewers in South Korea," highlighting that "a single gesture went beyond political language" as "the theatrics conveyed messages of trust that language alone could not."[28] These commentaries illustrated the paradoxical characteristics of

FIG. 5.2. South Korean president Moon Jae-in and North Korean leader Kim Jong-un meet in the truce village of Panmunjom. Korea Summit Press Pool / Pool via Reuters.

North Korea's charm offensive: although most elements of the charm offensive were described as extensively rehearsed performances, there were several unexpected scenes, moments of "restaging" that were extensively circulated by the media. These surprise moments highlighted Kim Jong-un and his team's personable aspects, supporting North Korea's goal to transform its international image.

Enhancing Charm and Relatability

Kim Jong-un drastically changed his public manners as part of his charm offensive. Similar to Iranian foreign minister Zarif, one of Kim's tools was smiling. Of the photos,

73 percent in Korean newspapers analyzed, and 82.4 percent in American newspapers analyzed, depicted Kim Jong-un and other high-profile North Korean leaders displaying a smile. Journalists also mentioned Kim's smiles in their respective articles. For instance, the *New York Times*' coverage of Kim's meeting with South Korea's special envoys noted that "the envoys were taken aback by Kim Jong-un's friendliness. . . . When it was time for farewells after a night of talk and dining, Mr. Kim walked them out and sent them off with smiles and waves."[29]

South Korean newspapers also discussed Kim Jong-un's "humble attitudes." *Chosun* emphasized that Kim showed honesty and respect toward President Moon when the two met during the inter-Korean summits.[30] An opinion piece by *Hankyoreh* captured Kim's polite manners, saying that "his use of honorific terms, smoking a cigarette outside the meeting spaces, and letting President Moon and his wife take the elevator first, were far from what we knew of Kim Jong-un as an arrogant, insolent young leader."[31] These humanizing descriptions contributed to his image as a relatable, even charming leader.

Distributed Charm—Enlisting Female "Ambassadors"

Kim Jong-un also delegated the task of seduction to close relatives. As part of his charm offensive, he enlisted female family members to emphasize a softened, "feminine" image of North Korea. Kim designated selected women as ambassadors of North Korea and created settings where they could shine the brightest in front of cameras.

Both the American and the South Korean press heavily reported about Hyon Song-wol, a famous North Korean singer and her all-female cheering squad when they were deployed to the PyeongChang Olympics. News articles often emphasized the explosive media attention given to Hyon, one commenting that such interest is almost becoming a "Hyon Song-wol syndrome."[32] Highlighting the news programs' constant close-ups of Hyon's face, articles mentioned that she is one of Kim Jong-un's people that are trained to be picture-perfect by displaying a "stylish and charismatic image," as one *Chosun* article put it.[33]

As part of his charm offensive, Kim Jong-un also enlisted his wife, Ri Sol-ju. While the First Lady title does not officially exist in North Korea, Kim elevated his wife's status from "comrade" to "First Lady" in 2018. By inviting Ri Sol-ju to his diplomatic meetings and international travels, including the inter-Korean summit, the visit to China, and the meeting with South Korean special envoys, Kim Jong-un used publicity to legitimize her title internationally. Journalists interpreted these moves as attempts to normalize North Korea as a "Western-like" state.[34] Ri Sol-ju quickly became a media sensation, as she walked in front of the cameras and held hands with her husband. Her beauty, attitudes, and fashion were lavishly covered by international media. The Kim couple was effectively treated as Western-style celebrities.

As mentioned before, Kim also enlisted his youngest sister, Kim Yo-jong, who was particularly suitable for this peculiar job. While Kim Yo-jong usually stayed behind the scenes in local politics, as North Korea's authoritarian regime required all propaganda to be concentrated on her brother, she was brought onstage as a lead actress when she came to the PyeongChang Winter Olympics. One article described her as a "nuclear bomb with a smile,"[35] another as serving as an emissary that sends a message to the world: "see, we're not that scary."[36]

Equalizing: Forging Sudden and Momentary Friendships

Lastly, North Korea's charm offensive involved communicating sudden "friendships" with "enemy nations," namely the United States and South Korea. As Kim's 2018 New Year's address started off by offering Seoul increased diplomatic communication, the North and South quickly built up a temporary amicable relationship, which one news source called "a sense of brotherliness."[37] The media suspected that North Korea's appeal to South Korea was a maneuver to drive a wedge between the United States and South Korea, but Kim Jong-un quickly reached out to the United States as well, suggesting a meeting with then president Trump. After this diplomatic gesture, the relationship between Donald Trump and Kim Jong-un drastically changed course. The South Korean *Chosun* mentioned that whereas Trump had called Kim a "mad man" only a few months earlier, he later referred to Kim as a "very open and very honorable man."[38] The *Wall Street Journal* similarly described this turnaround as "from name calling to high hopes."[39]

North Korea's charm offensive also presented North Korea and the United States as equal partners. Kim Jong-un aimed to demonstrate that his nation's power in some ways equals that of the United States. The *New York Times*' coverage of the Trump-Kim summit illustrates this effort:

All of the pageantry pointed to a meeting between two equals—from the row of American and North Korean flags that stood behind the leaders as they first met, to the joint entrance into the room where they signed a declaration.[40]

At the same time, news articles often depicted this sudden friendship as unstable and temporary. Journalists indicated that it rested on mutual benefits rather than on shared values. Kim's intention for this friendship was read as an attempt to lift or limit the economic sanctions against North Korea, whereas President Trump's enthusiastic response was interpreted as a maneuver to shift attention away from his administration's failing foreign policy in the Middle East.[41]

The Reception of North Korea's Charm Offensive— Journalistic Attitudes in the South Korean and American Press

To dig a little deeper into the media coverage of Kim Jong-un's charm offensive and to provide nuance, it is worth comparing the charm offensive's American and South Korean reception. In South Korea there was no uniform coverage of the events, as the media's reception of North Korea's charm offensive was partisan in tone. Conservative outlets tended to doubt Kim's intentions, and liberal outlets showed more support for North Korea's shifting diplomacy and for the Moon administration's cautiously open attitudes toward the North.

As part of the conservative media landscape, *Chosun* frequently quoted conservative political leaders in South Korea, the United States, and Japan, who were generally skeptical of

North Korea's diplomatic actions. These quotes mainly stated that Kim Jong-un's softened gestures toward South Korea were designed to drive the United States and South Korea further apart,[42] or to disguise North Korea's continuing nuclear program.[43] *Chosun*'s coverage of Kim Jong-un often showed him as a brutal, merciless, and war-loving despot, calling him "a slaughterer who even executed his own uncle, Jang Sung-taek and assassinated his stepbrother, Kim Jong-nam."[44] Such emphasis on Kim Jong-un's alienating characteristics was to caution readers from "being seduced by his words and actions."[45] Articles also condemned liberal media outlets for portraying Kim Jong-un in a positive light.[46]

In contrast, news articles from the liberal-leaning *Hankyoreh* reflected a more supportive sentiment. Many articles referred to North Korea's shifting diplomacy as an opportunity to improve the North-South Korean relationship, evaluating the current diplomatic thaw as a hopeful sign for peace. For example, an opinion piece commented that North Korea's participation in the PyeongChang Olympics "is a door to peace."[47] *Hankyoreh* increasingly depicted Kim Jong-un in a favorable light, describing him as "a practical leader,"[48] "open and confident,"[49] "honest and bold,"[50] "large-hearted,"[51] and "personable and relatable."[52] These articles also emphasized that ordinary South Koreans' perception of North Korea and Kim Jong-un has drastically changed since the North's conciliatory gestures (journalists aimed to prove this assertion by inserting quotes from South Korean citizens). *Hankyoreh*'s attitude toward North Korea's charm offensives was somewhat conflicted as journalists also claimed there was little possibility that people would be heavily affected by North Korea's diplomatic maneuvers.

American journalists also covered Kim's charm offensive in varying tones. Journalists sometimes expressed caution over his radical image makeover. Especially in the conservative-leaning *Wall Street Journal*, North Korea's acts were mainly understood as deceitful tactics that hid his true intentions. Journalists often criticized liberal outlets for glamorizing and giving excessive attention to North Korea's recent diplomatic move. For instance, an article commented that "gullible Western media . . . went ga-ga for the North Korean cheerleaders"[53] and that "the media went into full fanboy mode."[54]

Although the *New York Times* and the *Washington Post* were somewhat less critical about North Korea's diplomatic strategies and occasionally described them with words that exoticized North Korea—for example, referring to Kim Yo-jong as a "sphinxlike"[55] woman who "flashes that mysterious smile"[56]—both news outlets also presented mixed attitudes toward North Korea. Most of the articles included skeptical voices, even when the headlines were sensational. For example, a *New York Times* article obsessed over Kim Yo-jong's appearance at the PyeongChang Olympics, but it also included the voice of anti–North Korea protesters in the South who were "horrified by the notion that Ms. Kim could lull South Koreans, or anyone else, into forgetting the North's repression and human rights abuses."[57] As this example suggests, a mixture of conflicting tones made it difficult to pinpoint a uniform sentiment reflected in the articles.

There was another important difference between the American and South Korean coverage. American news outlets were keen on presenting North Korea's image change as an unexpected and radical shift. Even though the charm offensive included carefully planned and prearranged events, the American media coverage centered on surprise. For instance, the *New York Times* enthusiastically reported that "almost overnight, with friendly smiles and messages of reconciliation, Ms. Kim managed to help soften her country's image among South Koreans."[58] Articles in the American press variously mentioned that North Korea "abruptly changed course,"[59] or experienced an "astonishing turn of events,"[60] or argued that we were seeing an "unexpected burst of diplomacy."[61] Kim Yo-jong's attendance at the Winter Olympics was reported as "something of a last-minute surprise, the result of a rapidly unfolding series of events that began Jan. 1."[62] North Korea's communication about potential high-level meetings with other countries was covered as "a diplomacy blitz,"[63] in which Kim Jong-un presented "a remarkable shift in tone."[64] In all these cases, the coverage's language centers on surprise.

In contrast, South Korean journalists mostly emphasized continuity. *Chosun* spoke of the "Kim family's traditional rhetoric and strategy"[65] and reminded readers of North Korea's past actions. For instance, quoting a Japanese newspaper, it emphasized that "there have been several South-North unified Olympic teams in the past. Every time it produced a 'softened atmosphere,' but North Korea did not stop developing its nuclear weapons. Peace is only a fantasy."[66]

There were also times when South Korean journalists expressed surprise, and their American colleagues emphasized continuity. For instance, the *Wall Street Journal* cautioned its readers that "these are standard North Korean shakedown techniques, honed to perfection by three generations of regime negotiators."[67] And the South Korean press occasionally joined the American celebration of abrupt change and surprise; for instance *Chosun* wrote about "North Korea's unexpected action,"[68] whereas *Hankyoreh* mentioned a "sudden attitude change" on the part of the North.[69]

The mostly different attitudes are likely due to a difference in historical knowledge of North Korean politics among American and South Korean audiences. Most South Korean journalists and readers are well versed in the complicated past of Korean relations and have a hard time seeing North Korean diplomatic maneuvers as "unexpected" and "magical." The more commercially minded American press is also historically more inclined to emphasize novelty to increase reader interest.

American journalists had used the term "charm offensive" in connection with North Korea before, but they started to mention it explosively in 2018, suggesting that they regarded "charm offensive" as a kind of a keyword of the situation. In the analyzed *New York Times* and *Wall Street Journal* articles, seventy of eighty-four articles mentioned "charm offensive." In contrast, only fifteen of 136 analyzed Korean articles mentioned charm offensive directly, and in ten of them, charm offensive was quoted from American media outlets or foreign individuals. Korean journalists were more inclined to use terms such as "appeasement offensive," "peace offensive," "image change," and "regime propaganda."

There could be multiple explanations for this difference. The focus of South Korean media was on the relationship between North and South Korea rather than on individual or national charm. The South Korean press generally applied more careful and skeptical terms than the American press did in their description of North Korea's shifting diplomacy. The American press often used dramatic words such as "charmed the world" and "seized the spotlight," whereas the

Korean press spoke of "softened gestures" and "wanting a conversation." Such contrast in word choice may come from the different historical relationships that the United States and South Korea have built with North Korea. South Korea has experienced similar appeasing moments with North Korea in the past, which then often shifted back to a more hostile relationship. These past memories have remained in the South Korean collective consciousness and likely trigger caution in the interpretation of conciliatory North Korean gestures. Similar historical and cultural reflexes do not hold the American press back from a kind of Hollywood celebrity coverage.

Concluding Thoughts on Charm Offensives

Kim Jong-un's charm offensive exhibited five key characteristics: increasing openness to news photography, meticulously planned image campaigns with occasional improvisation, enhancement of his relatability, enlisting female "ambassadors," and forging sudden and momentary friendships with other political leaders. All these elements of Kim's charm offensive were concerted efforts to move North Korea's image from "villain" to "hero," or from "enemy" to "partner." Gaining prominence on the global media stage, Kim was able to communicate novel messages about his country and momentarily capture the imagination of his Western audience. Whether these changes in appearance bring anything in substance remains to be seen. But even capturing the Western media's attention with well-crafted political performances was a major feat for the North Korean regime. With a concerted and strategic charm offensive, Kim controlled more elements of the Western media coverage than Western journalists probably would like to admit. By opening up to the cameras, introducing previously rarely seen family members, and organizing visually spectacular events, Kim created the framework in which the Western media's coverage operated.

At the same time, he could not control all elements of the reception. "Charm offensive" was a term favored by the Western media, and the South Korean press handled the story with only a rare reference to the concept—illustrative of very different political stances, perspectives, and expectations of the American and South Korean media. Even the term "charm offensive" is missing in the Korean language. Since leading American news publications offer limited coverage of foreign affairs, American journalists were more likely to inflate the novelty and unexpectedness of Korean events to capture the audience's attention. Their South Korean colleagues could not escape strong skepticism given their audience's familiarity with previous failed reconciliation efforts with the North. And Kim's charm offensive triggered both enchantment and anxiety even on the side of American journalists. American journalists acknowledged the seductive powers of Kim's image campaign, but also referred to its potential to deceive.

Although North Korea was successful in capturing the global audience's attention in the beginning of 2018, skepticism toward North Korea's diplomatic tactics has been growing ever since. The United States and North Korea have not agreed on the steps of denuclearization since the Singapore summit. North Korea continues to communicate a dual message of threat and charm. Another US–North Korea summit was again held in February 2019 in Hanoi, and Kim Jong-un and President Trump had a surprise meeting at the demilitarized zone in June 2019. In November 2022, Kim Jong-un oversaw the firing of a new type of intercontinental ballistic missile. This threatening move was combined with a strange charm offensive, as he was bringing his young daughter to the event. As of the writing of this chapter, American–North Korean relations are tense, and Kim's charm offensive seems like a moment from a faraway past. The American–North Korean summits are increasingly regarded as failures. It seems that Kim's charm offensive was a brief moment of surprise, and for many, hope, that quickly faded away.

We are likely to see even more charm offensives in foreign affairs in the future. The global proliferation of photographs and videos on social media may inspire political leaders to turn to charm offensives as these strategic public relations campaigns offer the chance of rapid and readily disseminated visual seduction. Whether charm offensives ultimately succeed or fail in shifting a country's image, they certainly manage to capture some of the shrinking space dedicated to foreign affairs reporting in contemporary news outlets.

Charm offensives can appear in a variety of forms; Zarif's charm offensive in 2015 and Kim Jong-un's in 2018 were only two among its many possible permutations. Journalists have used the term "charm offensive" in connection with the Chinese delegation's efforts to woo investors in Davos in 2024; with the Australian foreign minister's frequent visits to the South Pacific region to compete with China; with Ukrainian president Zelensky's videos on social media after Russia's invasion of Ukraine in 2022; and with Turkish president Erdogan's friendlier gestures toward the EU and Egypt in 2020, just to name a few. Charm offensives also transcend ideological boundaries, from the charm offensives of the illiberal Hungarian prime minister Orbán to the post-ideological French president Macron to the liberal American president Biden. Some of these charm offensives were presented in a positive light, for instance Jacinda Ardern's serious efforts to improve relations with the Maori, while others were described as diplomatic disasters, like Canadian prime minister Justin Trudeau and his family's overuse of Indian clothing during their visit to India.[70]

While the range of charm offensives is wide, there are also strong commonalities among them. They are all performed both for diplomatic counterparts and for the international media, aiming to alter preexisting perceptions of a country. They use tools of mediated friendliness in the form of amicable gestures like smiles and embraces and flattering words. And they tend to have a focus on leaders instead of policies, institutions, or other significant forms of political action. A charm offensive is "charming" because it escapes the strictly rational and instrumental, and because it is not easily tamed by definition-loving academics. Still, understanding how strategic charm offensives operate is crucial to conceptualizing diplomacy in the twenty-first century.

6

Authenticity without Charm

GERMAN CHANCELLOR
ANGELA MERKEL

Before Christmas in 2020, a holiday marked by the ongoing coronavirus pandemic, German chancellor Angela Merkel gave an emotionally charged speech. She begged Germans to follow official guidance on social distancing. She even referred to grandparents for whom this might be the last Christmas if viewers did not take proper precautions. The speech would have been standard for any of the "charming" politicians discussed in this book. But not for Merkel. Raw display of emotion is not what she is known for at home or abroad. This authenticity performance was noticed and remembered because it was deeply unexpected from Merkel. This chapter is thus dedicated to a "countercase": when a political leader builds authenticity without regularly deploying the strategies and tricks of charm. A charming performance always needs to be perceived as authentic, yet an authentic performance—perhaps surprisingly—can sometimes work without the qualities of charm.

Angela Merkel was elected as chancellor of Germany in 2005, and she remained in power for four consecutive elections, spending a whopping sixteen years in this influential political role. When she left the office in December 2021—after a challenging phase of pandemic waves, a devastating flood in Germany, and political turmoil in Afghanistan—support for her performance was at 80 percent,[1] a popularity level almost no politician reaches these days. Families had named their children after her,[2] "the free world" had come to rely on Merkel as its new leader during the Trump administration,[3] and she was lauded for navigating the pandemic with outstanding efficiency.[4] Some people criticized her approach during the 2015 refugee crisis, but even her critics would acknowledge her extensive experience and knowledge of contemporary political affairs.

Things looked less promising when Merkel first entered politics in the newly united federal republic in the 1990s. She had come from East Germany, and her political success was anything but certain in this new and very male-dominated environment. Her 2005 victory against incumbent Gerhard Schröder came as an absolute surprise to many. However, as she established herself, the media adjusted representations in a way that scholars termed "the Merkel effect": her country of origin faded into the background, while her political power became the factor defining her coverage.[5] With her consistent use of a diamond-shaped hand gesture (fig. 6.1), she became a reliable and predictable presence on the global stage. Internationally, Merkel was even framed as an icon against the rising tide of populism.[6] She embodied persistence in unpredictable global politics.

FIG. 6.1. "Queen Elizabeth II receives Chancellor Merkel in a private audience at Windsor Castle." Posted by @bundeskanzlerin on Instagram, July 2, 2021.

The first woman to ever become a German chancellor, Merkel had built a reputation for rational decision making and skilled negotiation. She has come to stand for expertise, efficiency, and pragmatism. She navigated an extremely turbulent and mediated political landscape without deploying techniques of the charming interaction. While she no doubt operated in the same attention economy as other politicians, she managed to carve out a radically different strategy to deal with it. Her self-representation was also in juxtaposition to the populist rhetoric that helped many other figures ascend to power globally during her administration.

The general reliance on social media to "personalize" politics posed a specific challenge to a politician who has always been devoted to rational sobriety. Where others used the opportunity to make their charm shine, what did a leader like Merkel do? How did her persona make such an unexpected and unusual mark? How did she go against preconceived notions such as the power of spectacle on social media or the power of personalization in global politics? Her Instagram account may hold some answers. While Instagram is particularly known for its visuality and emotional appeal, Merkel seemed to carve out a nonspectacular persona there, over time effectively ignoring the platform's social and cultural norms. Merkel's Instagram profile—much in line with her general public presentation—stood out in consistency and ordinariness, while regularly dropping any intimate qualities. Instead of adapting her visuals to social media's logic, Merkel shaped social media to effectively host her spectacle-free and expertise-focused persona.

The Evolution of Merkel's "Authenticity without Charm" Approach on Social Media

Social media have never been a natural habitat for Angela Merkel. She was a latecomer to Instagram, opening the account only as the platform had clearly outpaced Facebook for a broader reach especially to younger audiences. The Instagram account @bundeskanzlerin was created on June 2, 2015, with an initial forty-five photographs from the past years posted. By the time Merkel stepped down as chancellor in November 2021, it had 1.8 million followers and 2,023 posts as well as about one hundred stories published. Merkel's team also regularly posted a video podcast, which was shared on the government's website as well as on her Instagram account. The videos showed Merkel from head to waist, talking straight to the camera usually with her hallmark diamond-shaped gesture. The podcast was an attempt to communicate political issues and government news in easily digestible chunks. But unlike many other politicians in this book, Merkel always made it clear that her social media presence was produced by a professional staff. She did not pretend to feel "natural" and "at home" in the posts, carefully avoiding any first-person communication in the captions.

The first phase of her Instagram account had an experimental character in style and content and lasted for about eighteen months starting from June 2015. Photos were aesthetically inventive, often using strong filters, unconventional lighting situations, and extreme perspectives. Few videos appeared at all. Architectural motifs and snapshots captured moods in and around the chancellery and Angela Merkel's travels. Interestingly, only about half of the pictures sampled from this first phase showed the chancellor, and under 5 percent showed her by herself. In these photographs, Merkel often appeared as a traditionally charismatic leader at a critical distance and almost exclusively with another person or in groups. The photos created an air of mystery and opaque power, following the chancellor in her everyday activities, but never giving away much about her personality. More than half of the photos from this phase provide a backstage feel, but not in the sense of how Ardern or Orbán weaponized the backstage. Merkel did not introduce her viewers to her family or other aspects of her private life. The focus, with some Instagram-style design, remained on the "office," just in a somewhat stylized form. The Instagram account initially was clearly approached within the logic of the platform, but without dropping the formal mask of politics.

By the end of 2016, the strategy seemed to shift, ushering in a new era of "consolidation." Videos started playing a bigger role, especially through the launch of Merkel's regular video podcast in April 2018. The number of likes also grew fast. The aesthetic quality shifted from filters, backlighting, and spectacular perspectives to a more formal style. Merkel now became the central motif of almost all photos. A pattern of showing her in diplomatic or conference situations emerged, and a culture of repetition, predictability, and reliability became firmly established. She was often presented in the company of other heads of state or celebrities like members of royal families or famous athletes, most commonly the German national soccer team. Overall, the account during this phase turned into a supplement to standard official reporting with events and situations of public interest depicted from a visually interesting, but still very official, formal, and distanced angle.

In the third phase, which began with the outbreak of Covid-19 in Germany in March 2020, the account strategy significantly shifted again. Merkel focused on a series of crises. The video format took over to form the majority of posts. Views grew to around two hundred thousand. These videos mostly followed the pattern of clear, straightforward transmission of information, with very few ritualistic elements. We see snippets of press conferences that deal with the pressing issues of her policy response to the ongoing coronavirus pandemic or other crises like a flood in western Germany or the Taliban's takeover in Afghanistan in 2021. The content is professionally produced and edited. Merkel is now depicted by herself and gazing right into the camera almost half of the time. This makes her appearances more obviously staged, but she is also more directly addressing the audience. We see almost no visuals that convey a backstage character. Rather, the account becomes a channel for crisis communication with Merkel playing the role of a leader and an expert communicating with her audience.

Overall, the strategy defining her Instagram account has been gradually adjusted and fitted onto Merkel's already-existing style of presentation and reputation—rather than Instagram as a platform reshaping her public persona. The Instagram account thus becomes "merkelized" over time, reproducing her formal, scripted, and information-driven style of speech and appearance. While there are slight differences across these various phases, what we see overall is a construction of strong political authenticity without regular attempts to charm.

The Visual Construction of Authenticity without Charm

While Merkel was experimenting with social media, her representation throughout adhered more to formal political conventions than to charming ones. She was presented as a somewhat distanced yet extraordinary leader, firmly and calmly in charge. For instance, a characteristic image showed Merkel descending the government's plane in Frankfurt in July 2015 (fig. 6.2). The photographer took the image from ground level, and its frame includes the rims of a luxury car on the left. The perspective and sharp contrasts in black and white give the photo a spectacular air. We see a second person, presumably a security employee in a suit. Shades add to the "coolness" and "VIP feel" of the scene. The photo is highly stylized, showing Merkel's everyday life from a backstage angle that emphasizes power and extraordinariness. In contrast to Jacinda Ardern, for whom the backstage angle

FIG. 6.2. "Chancellor #Merkel exiting the government's aircraft on her way to the day of senior citizens (#Seniorentag) in #Frankfurt." Posted by @bundeskanzlerin on Instagram, July 2, 2015.

brought proximity, Merkel remains at a distance, signaling a charismatic leader rather than a charming politician. Intimacy and ordinariness are outweighed by a distant presentation. She emerges as authentically distant and reserved, more as a gray bureaucrat than a seductive charmer.

In another characteristic image, Merkel is in conversation with Russian president Vladimir Putin (fig. 6.3). The photo was posted in August 2018. At that time conflicts dominated German-Russian relations, and the media scrutinized Merkel's stance toward Russia. This photo shows the two sitting in an almost perfectly symmetrical, friendly, and sunlit setup at a garden table. Merkel's jacket blends in with the background. The two powerful politicians, both seated, look at each other intently and seriously. Merkel speaks and

bundeskanzlerinmerkel ● Follow ···
Schloss Meseberg

bundeskanzlerinmerkel ● Heute ist Präsident Putin zu Gast bei Kanzlerin Merkel. Die Themen: die Lage in der Ukraine, der Gastransit nach Europa, der Syrien-Konflikt, das iranische Atomprogramm und die deutsch-russischen Beziehungen. „Auch kontroverse Themen können nur im Gespräch gelöst werden. Und deshalb freue ich mich, heute Wladimir Putin hier zu Gast zu haben", so die Kanzlerin. --- Today

32,929 likes
AUGUST 18, 2018

Log in to like or comment.

FIG. 6.3. "Today, Russia's President Putin is visiting Chancellor Merkel in Meseberg, at the guest house of the Federal Government. The topics: the situation in Ukraine, gas transfer to Europe, the conflict in Syria, Iran and the bilateral relations. 'Even controversial problems can only be solved by talks. Therefore, I am happy to welcome President Putin,' Chancellor Merkel said. #putin #merkel #diplomacy #diplomatie #diplogram #zusammenarbeit #cooperation." Posted by @bundeskanzlerin on Instagram, August 18, 2018.

gestures moderately as Putin listens, holding on to his glass of water. Merkel is presented as in charge here, as speaker and host to this professional yet intimate encounter. Again, the image communicates a bit of a background feel, but within the boundaries of professional politics. It is a visual piece of diplomacy showing Merkel's dedication to reason and argument, while depicting the encounter as generally friendly and receptive. Interestingly, while Merkel is being intimate with other politicians, including with adversaries, she is specifically not being intimate with the camera and the viewer. Intimacy is reserved for interpersonal encounters; mediation is treated with distrust.

Crises always foreground the leader, offering opportunities to present relatable moments. Crises also provide chances for the politician to fuse with her audience as a leader and at the same time member of a traumatized community. But during the biggest crisis of Merkel's political career, the coronavirus pandemic in 2020, her image was still closer to a bureaucratic representation than to a charming one. Her communication was dominated by regular and popular video podcasts, visually resembling the many snippets from press conferences and parliamentary statements posted during that period. For her agitated audience, which was shaken by the global pandemic, Merkel offered a reliable and reassuring presence, consistent and predictable.

We often see Merkel standing or sitting, frontally facing the camera. On one of the images a formal press statement background is framed with a flag to the left, but a slight lack of lighting and sharpness still give this image a somewhat amateurish feel (fig. 6.4). Fully committed to the transmission of information, black all-caps font is layered on white lines across Merkel's chest, underlining her speech. While the textual content is tragic, the visual presentation is perfectly plain, almost generic. Merkel's facial expressions are bordering on boredom and seem to contradict the immediacy and emergency of her words. She seems to signal that while the world is in crisis, there is absolutely nothing to fear. Watching Merkel's regular Instagram video posts thus gives visual respite from the fast-paced changes and risks "out there" in the world. This is hardly an immediate, passionate, ad hoc reaction of a real person, but rather a professional office speaking to its well-defined audience.

In another image we see an even stronger level of stagedness (fig. 6.5). The occasion of the photograph is a formal

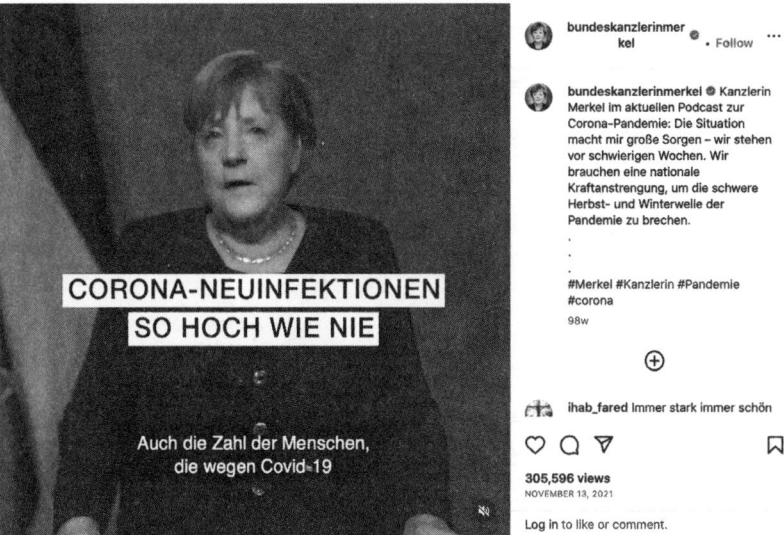

FIG. 6.4. "Chancellor Merkel in the latest podcast on the Covid pandemic: The situation worries me a lot—We are facing difficult weeks. We need a serious national effort to break the severe wave of infections this fall and winter. #Merkel #Kanzlerin #Pandemie #corona." Posted by @bundeskanzlerin on Instagram, November 13, 2021.

handing over of a ministry in May 2021. The photo shows former and incoming ministers, the president, who is in charge of representative tasks, and Chancellor Merkel. The four figures are neatly lined up in Bellevue Palace in Berlin. All four face the camera with their feet close together and hands clutched in front of them. The colors are bright and low saturation, almost resembling the sterile interiors of a hospital or a drab office, with Merkel's blue jacket being the most colorful feature. The stiff formality of the image almost has a satirical effect. But the visual emphasis on stillness is also a hint at stability. The almost military

FIG. 6.5. "Today, President Frank-Walter Steinmeier discharged
Franziska Giffey from her office as federal minister for family
affairs, senior citizens, women, and youth and appointed Attorney
General Christine Lambrecht additionally as federal minister
for family affairs. Chancellor Merkel attended the delivery of the
discharge and appointment certificates in Bellevue castle." Posted
by @bundeskanzlerin on Instagram, May 20, 2021.

discipline displayed by the politicians conveys a sense of
reason and control. The depiction of Merkel repeats the format of the video podcasts with her frontal positioning and
formal pose. The group photo simply extends the frame to
include her surroundings. The orientation toward the viewer
makes this presentation look staged, while it also communicates a sense of public service mentality. Consistency governs
representation.

Lastly of these types of images, it is important to return
to the most popular post ever published on Merkel's Instagram account, which was mentioned as the opening of this
chapter (fig. 6.6). It is a video snippet of a parliamentary
address on December 9, 2020, arguing for a quick and effective decision on how to run or not run schools in the days

bundeskanzlerinmerkel ✓ • Follow

bundeskanzlerinmerkel ✓ Die nächsten Tage werden nicht einfach. Kanzlerin Merkel ruft im Bundestag dazu auf, sie gemeinsam durchzustehen und die Kontakte im Kampf gegen die Corona-Pandemie weiter zu reduzieren.

#kanzlerin #bundeskanzlerin #merkel #corona #pandemie #coronapandemie #weihnachten #bundestag #covid_19

146w

chocine19 Die selbstgemachte und selbsternannte Pandemie die gar keine ist. Durch MEdien hochgepusht zu

1,629,260 views
DECEMBER 9, 2020

Log in to like or comment.

für diese drei Tage doch irgendeine Lösung zu finden?

FIG. 6.6. "The coming days won't be easy. Chancellor Merkel calls for a unified effort to weather through them and further reduce contacts in the fight against the COVID pandemic. #kanzlerin #bundeskanzlerin #merkel #corona #pandemie #coronapandemie #weihnachten #bundestag #covid_19." Posted by @bundeskanzlerin on Instagram, December 9, 2020.

before Christmas to reduce the risk of contagion over the holidays. The post clocked a record of 1.6 million views. Yet, even in this exceptional case of "emotionality" by Merkel, the visual qualities of the video are strikingly minimalistic. Merkel is behind the Bundestag's speaker's podium, marked by the logo in front and two microphones to the side. She is sporting a red version of her signature jacket and gesticulates emphatically as she emphasizes the importance of a fast decision on schooling. There is nothing visually appealing or exciting about the scene. It is formal, and static—again almost generic. Merkel's performance resonates most in absolute ordinariness rather than in spectacle. She is the most successful in building on consistency rather than on surprise.

What is overall missing in the representation of Merkel on social media? At least four techniques of the "charming interaction" are curiously lacking here: demasking, breaking from routine, restaging, and equalizing. She is not inviting the viewer to explore her private life; she does not reveal the backstage of politics to us; she does not show vulnerability; she is not creating spectacular pseudo-events for us; and she is definitely not dropping the formal role of a leader to appear as our next-door neighbor. Nothing could be further from her than to ask us to find the owner of a toy bunny at an airport. She remains the predictable, reliable, and consistent Angela Merkel, long-term chancellor of Germany, even when she enters the unpredictable and passionate war zone of social media.

Occasional Attempts at Charm

Yet, there are some exceptions, when even Angela Merkel attempted to play with something that vaguely resembles charm. On some rare occasions, Merkel's Instagram did attempt to portray her with the contemporary tools of charming seduction. These exceptions offer a window to look at the possibilities of presenting Merkel in a charming light. The possibility did exist, yet she and her team chose otherwise.

FIG. 6.7. "#Shoes of Chancellor Angela Merkel and British Prime Minister Theresa #May." Posted by @bundeskanzlerin on Instagram, July 20, 2016.

One Instagram image shows an unconventional close-up of the shoes of British prime minister Theresa May and Angela Merkel standing on a podium in July 2016 (fig. 6.7). May's bare legs in leopard-patterned heels clearly stand out from the gray carpet—and from the plain black slippers and black pants of Angela Merkel beside them. The photo delicately communicates the powerful onstage position uniting the two women while simultaneously emphasizing the differences between them. The contrast between the two also highlights Merkel's unsophisticated and distinctively not typically feminine presentation, offering a male-like depiction.[7] This is an authenticity performance of a very different sort. It emphasizes Merkel's everyday-ness and groundedness, but compares it with a more sensual and attractive mainstream "femininity." The image is humorous, self-deprecating. While being in sync with the visual expectations of Instagram, the image still does not follow conventions of political personalization, as it cuts

bundeskanzlerinmerkel · Follow ···
South Tyrol

bundeskanzlerinmerkel ● In weniger als 14 Tagen beginnt die #WM2018. Kanzlerin Merkel war heute im Trainingslager in Südtirol um dem @DFB_Team viel Glück und Erfolg für die hoffentlich erfolgreiche Titelverteidigung zu wünschen. --- In a couple of days the World Cup begins. Chancellor Merkel was in the training camp in South Tyrol today to wish the team good luck and success for the

♡ ◯ ▽   🔖

21,837 likes
JUNE 3, 2018

Log in to like or comment.

FIG. 6.8. "In a couple of days the World Cup begins. Chancellor Merkel was in the training camp in South Tyrol today to wish the team good luck and success for the hopefully successful title defense. #DieMannschaft #fußball #football #nationalmannschaft #teamgeist." Posted by @bundeskanzlerin on Instagram, June 3, 2018.

out most of Merkel's body and persistently communicates the message of "predictability" rather than "charm." The scene is fully staged. Yet, it communicates an authentic Merkel, who remains herself in an ever-changing and increasingly sexualized mediated landscape.

Another example shows Merkel with a group of German national soccer team athletes as they prepare for the World Championship in summer 2018 (fig. 6.8). Merkel frequently met soccer players and athletes, enthusiastically cheering at world championships. In these meetings, Merkel used body language regularly associated with male politicians. We see Merkel in an unusually pronounced masculine pose here too, as she leans forward, resting her elbows on spread knees, mirroring German soccer goalkeeper Manuel Neuer, sitting across from her. The atmosphere is informal and jovial—the athletes and Merkel are laughing and chatting. None of the depicted are looking into the camera. The photographer seems to peek in from a door with a bit of the door frame captured in the lower-left corner. Such depictions certainly try to bring Merkel closer to the viewer. Yet, she still seems to keep the "mask" on in these occasions, wearing her formal outfit and radiating an aura of respect. She does not allow a moment of "demasking" unlike the other politicians discussed in this book. There is nothing spectacular or backstage-like about the scene, even if Merkel appears as more relatable. Her representation is also following long-held conventions around male politicians interacting with sportsmen. She fully adheres to these gendered norms of interaction.

Research on Merkel has shown that she has regularly received positive feedback from the press whenever she has followed male-dominated expectations of political behavior, pushing her gender into the background.[8] Since most political examples globally were still coming from male politicians, Merkel was following the patterns that were available, without consciously pushing or shifting them. She was rewarded when her representation matched with the established expectations. If we compare her with Ardern, both navigated their roles in very restrictive gendered environments. Yet Ardern made the impossible expectations visible, even occasionally commenting or ridiculing them, if not necessarily challenging them. Merkel refrained from any discussion of gender and regularly appeared as yet another male politician on the global stage, which, by the way, she would not regard as a stage, refusing theatrics and performance.

In some rare cases, Merkel attempted a combined "restaging" and "demasking," moving her interactions outside of expected settings, and attempting to appear as "one

FIG. 6.9. "Hello 'Wirbelwind,' newborn calf at the farm of family Trede in northern Germany. Chancellor Merkel met them during a debate on TV, followed [*sic*] their invitation today—and chose a name for the calf. #farming #bauernhof #landwirtschaft #agriculture." Posted by @bundeskanzlerin on Instagram, July 19, 2018.

of us." A characteristic example was her visit to a farm in Schleswig-Holstein in 2018, where she named a newborn calf (fig. 6.9). But even here, instead of sporting a casual outfit, she came to the stable in her regular red jacket looking as formal and elegant as she does at a high-level European Union meeting. The outcome was a somewhat awkward scene: an elite professional somehow transported for a moment to an odd setting, appearing visibly uncomfortable in the interaction. We saw the "regular" Merkel, just displaced. No private, informal side appeared. There was no chance for the audience to fuse with the performance as the performance's elements appeared completely disjointed and manufactured. Admittedly, there was some authenticity in the awkwardness.

Concluding Thoughts on Authenticity without Charm

Merkel offers a strong case for the possibility of appearing authentic without the strategies of charm. She built a political persona on predictability and expertise, without appearing as an intimate friend. She managed to take this path even in the contemporary action-filled and spectacle-focused media environment. Instead of shaping her online persona according to the traditions and needs of the popular platform Instagram, Merkel bent Instagram to host her unique persona. The expected "charming" side of authenticity was neglected, leaving us with an approach that conveyed authenticity as well as rationality. Attempts at performing intimacy were briefly present in the earliest phase of her Instagram account but were swiftly removed to shift from an Instagram pattern of presentation (elusive and mood centered) to a "Merkel-ized" pattern of presentation (transparent and information centered). The idiosyncrasy of this approach to Instagram culture becomes especially salient when compared to other leaders' social media use, including the ones presented in this book's previous chapters, which mobilize charm and relatability to gain sympathy.[9] This book began with Jacinda Ardern, another strong female politician on the global stage, whose approach could not have been more different. Yet both politicians astutely managed the dangerous waters of global politics.

Merkel thus presents a case when an internationally significant political player remains successful over almost two decades, without adhering to dominant expectations of "charm" in the new media environment. Merkel proves that authenticity without charm is a possible strategy for politicians, even in the new, instant, and visually excessive media ecology of the twenty-first century. This finding challenges the view that politics is always built on personalization and that social media are exclusively focused on relatability, spectacle, and drama.

But Germany might be a unique historical case. The country had an exceptionally negative experience with charisma during World War II, as Adolf Hitler weaponized his charisma to perpetrate genocide against the Jewish people and other targeted populations. Weber's classical theory of charisma, with which I began this book, is often condemned for allowing a positive interpretation of charismatic and fascistic leadership, even though his theory predated Hitler. Interestingly, distrust toward charisma has opened up a unique space in Germany for an expert leader that may not be fully replicable elsewhere. With a focus on deception and not seduction, German publics tend to push back when personal magnetism appears again on the political stage.

Recently, American sociologist Robin Wagner-Pacifici argued that American president Biden exhibits qualities that amount to a special category of leadership that she terms "anticharisma."[10] After the turbulent years of the Trump administration, with a style many voters found destructive and divisive rather than classically charismatic, Biden's steady and empathetic politics won the US elections in 2020. Only time will tell whether the emergence of similar leaders worldwide remains a possibility or whether Germany offers a truly unique historical and cultural environment for anticharming leadership that we just cannot find as often elsewhere.

7

The Power of Charm in Global Politics

A BALANCING ACT BETWEEN SEDUCTION AND DECEPTION

This book presents charm as a key feature of politics world-wide. With our increased focus on personalities in a highly visual and immediate media environment, magnetic person-alities will regularly capture our hearts, minds, and politics on the global stage. The future of democracy will be shaped by the elusive quality of charm more than we care to admit. Charm has the power to bring good to the world in the best sense of seduction, but it can also take the form of deception, or even abuse, if weaponized for the wrong cause. Under-standing this duality is essential when describing the role of personal magnetism in contemporary public life.

On the positive side, which is often neglected, an appeal-ing personality can bring politics closer to exhausted or indifferent audiences worldwide. A leader with a charming personality can make us think that he or she indeed delivers the "change we can believe in." When attention is scattered and media platforms are fragmented, a personality can serve as an icon, a symbolic condensation of complex policies and laws. The gray, establishment aura of "old" parties can get a powerful image makeover through a charming and relatable personality. This personality can shake up the scene and usher in a new era, at least temporarily. Generations of social scientists were taught that charisma and bureaucracy are competitors in a forever quest for power.[1] But in reality charm now permeates nearly every aspect of politics. Even gray bureaucrats rally behind magnetic politicians. Just consider the Democratic Party's quick seduction by Barack Obama, who swiftly became the president of the United States, or all the charmless EU bureaucrats who line up to take selfies with Ukrainian president Zelensky. We live in a new era of politics, when exhibiting or being close to the stardust of charm strongly defines political power.

In this book I have described techniques that politicians use to manufacture charm in the media. I particularly focused on five: authenticity performance (when politicians adjust their behaviors to appear as "real" and relatable to their audiences); demasking (which refers to politicians' attempts to remove their official masks to display either vulnerability or strength); breaking from routine (politicians' interruption of the flow of time to create minor, substitute "pseudo-events" for the media); restaging (when politicians create a controlled environment and space, an ideal stage for their charm to shine through); and equalizing (when politicians present diverse audiences as a coherent community). All these methods, and potentially many more, bring faraway politicians closer to their audiences. In ideal cases, the performers fuse with their distant and varied audiences, leading to successful political and social performances.

But there is no doubt a darker side to charm. Charm is linked to trauma and the excessive desire to please. A biography of American president John F. Kennedy reminds the reader that Kennedy at the age of two had to spend three months in a sanatorium, without his parents, recovering from scarlet fever. Here, the little Jack "demonstrated the first signs of what would be a lifelong ability to attract attention by *charming* others. He so captivated his nurse that it was reported that she begged to be allowed to stay with him."[2] Charm here becomes a coping mechanism, used as a tool for survival and love. This is a well-described process in contemporary childhood trauma research.[3]

Charm can also be weaponized in the service of abuse. Domestic abusers regularly turn to charm to make us stay in situations when we should really leave. Abusers often play a game of duality: one day appearing as charming, the next day torturing our souls and bodies. Most accounts of American sex offender and financier Jeffrey Epstein highlight exactly this duality in his actions. Epstein seduced many victims at the beginning with his personal magnetism and with promises of prestigious scholarships and fancy trips, just to trap them, abuse them, and ruin their lives.[4] This dual technique might explain why charming abusers are often tolerated, in private and public life, until it is too late.

Just as charming abusers can wreck our domestic lives, charming personalities can also destroy our politics. With our attention dedicated to mesmerizing personalities, we might forget that much of what matters in our political lives lacks spark, glitter, and spectacle. Charm can limit our capacity to see other valuable political qualities. Some of the most influential politicians in history did not possess any personal magic, and yet they were able to deliver.[5] In contrast, some of the most horrendous political and human disasters were linked to charisma, which remains a key feature of fascist and authoritarian leadership.

Countries' public relations campaigns in the form of "charm offensives" will characterize international diplomacy more than ever. This book analyzed two examples in detail: Iran's charm offensive during the 2015 nuclear deal negotiations and North Korea's charm offensive in relation to the Winter Olympics in 2018. Brief charm offensives, when charm is weaponized for a particular political goal on the global stage, will be frequently employed to capture the attention of domestic and international audiences. They will be particularly popular with authoritarian and illiberal regimes that will need a quick image makeover in the Western media.

All this raises the question of whether we are going to have more charming leaders in the future. Is the game of charm the most important gamble of our political lives today? It would be easy to give the grim answer that all we are going to see in the future is charm, nothing but charm, just in various shades and colors. But the truth is that contemporary politics and media still allowed the emergence of Angela Merkel. Expertise, empathy, predictability, and good old efficiency are still valued, even in the current age.[6] A powerful performance of professionalism occasionally still breaks the magic spell of charm. Charm, while a frequent marker of political success, is by no means the only way to achieve legitimacy, authenticity, and power. Many of the crucial skills needed for successful politics, such as carefulness, patience, dedication, perseverance, and a sense of duty, are not connected to charm but are sometimes still acknowledged by voters.

A likely scenario may be an oscillation between moments of charm and moments of "plainness." Societies for periods of time will look for and appreciate a charming leader, even if abusive, but in a moment of disillusionment might turn to a less spectacular, less entertaining leader who is perceived as the one who will get the job done. And less charismatic and charming leaders could very well be replaced at the next elections, if a contender who is perceived to have personal magnetism decides to run. A cyclical process of charm / no charm is the most likely scenario, as societies, similarly to human bodies, seek renewal and change.

Margaret Canovan, analyzing the rise of populism worldwide, argued that democracy has two faces: a "pragmatic" and a "redemptive" one.[7] Pragmatically, democracy is basically a form of peaceful conflict resolution. But many seek more than simple institutional functioning and bureaucratic peace. This leads us to the "redemptive" function: the filling of the shell of democracy with revolutionary content. While many see populism as simply a pathology, a type of illness we need to remove as swiftly as possible, it is possible to look at populism as a chance for change and renewal. Perhaps charm functions like this. The dramatic breakthrough of personality in the form of a "charm attack" can shake the calm foundations of politics and invigorate change, serving ultimately a redemptive function. But institutional balance will require a swing back to times of peace, and the charming performer will often be replaced by an efficient bureaucrat with regulated emotions.

We will also see charming moments within noncharming administrations. Even in the case of noncharming politicians, we can find strong attempts to bring them closer to their audiences. As I am writing this conclusion, President Biden has just met with Xi Jinping, his Chinese counterpart, in person to resolve differences. No doubt this meeting could have been arranged online, faraway from intrusive cameras. Yet, both leaders found it important to display the power of personal magnetism to emphasize the enduring importance of an in-person, emphatically not virtual handshake. Similarly, why did Secretary of State Antony Blinken need to visit Israel and Arab states after Hamas's 2023 attacks when rockets were still flying? Because in-person handshakes and listening still matter, even in war zones. These are the moments when personal magnetism and empathy can directly shine through and spread to the world through visual representations. Despite President Biden's limited "celebrity charm," social media are still flooded with memes endowing him with superhero powers, especially at high-stake negotiations, again highlighting the need to construct charm when there is little to find. And even in Biden's case, there are elements of charm: his warmth, his very human sympathy with personal distress and trauma, his believable smile. It might not be "charm" exactly, but something genuinely human is there.

There will also be cases when polarizing figures will be perceived as exceptionally charming by certain audiences, while being characterized as the ultimate villain by others. A recent example could be the global clash of narratives over Prince Harry and his wife, Meghan Markle, who left the British royal family and started a new life in California. While many embrace them as the charming icons of a new era of diversity and renewal in royal life and global philanthropy, others attack them relentlessly as frauds and traitors who disrespect British royal tradition. While their charm and magnetism clearly work for certain audiences, the other side remains unconvinced. We will clash over iconic figures, and through these disagreements, we will clarify what we stand for in politics and public life.[8]

Given that charm is ultimately the outcome of cultural evaluation, no leader will be perceived as charming or charismatic by everyone. Especially those who have extensive personal experiences with the political leader might emphasize that his or her public image of charm is ultimately fraudulent. Mary L. Trump, the niece of President Trump, shared a powerful moment of debunked charm in her book. In April 2017, a few months after her uncle became president, Mary L. Trump received an invitation to a family celebration at the White House. As guests arrived, President Trump was meeting them at the doorway. He greeted his niece with the exclamation: "I especially asked for you to be here." In Mary Trump's interpretation, that "was the kind of thing he often said to charm people, and he had a knack for tailoring his comment to the occasion, which was all the more impressive because I knew it wasn't true."[9] In this case the attempt to charm spectacularly failed as the targeted receiver immediately perceived it as fake.

Charm will not define all politicians and political interactions, but ignoring charm would be a grave mistake. Let's face it: we live in an age of stardust and charm. With political personalization happening on a variety of platforms globally, the performed personality of politicians matters more than ever before. Whether we highlight charm's negative or positive features, it is—and will be—a crucial form of political power. The current visual and networked media environment in which politicians operate coupled with a lower loyalty to parties both point to an era when charm and charisma will be defining features of our public lives. When images of politicians quickly reach us, even internationally, these visuals will no doubt shape our political behavior. And with the growing distrust of facts, personalities might gain a stronger traction than ever. We have always filtered facts based on whether we trust the person who uttered them.[10] Now that personalities are increasingly in the forefront in international media, their role in shaping what constitutes "facts" will be fundamental.

Let me end the book on a personal note. Recently I attended a memorial service of a dear family member. The old man's daughter spoke beautifully of her late father, trying to capture his personality in a few sentences:

> A gentleman and a gentle man, Dad was someone who, just by being in his presence made you feel that you were special, unique and a gift. Magnetically, he drew people to him—not for sage advice or loquacious conversation, but for the way he made you feel. Valued. Worthy. Wanted. Included. Accepted. Loved.[11]

At the time of the memorial service, I had been struggling for some years to define charm. And suddenly, there it was, right in front of me. These sentences included almost everything about charm I collected over many years of research. They summarized charm's magic both for the performer and for his audience and highlighted charm's exceptional power for our lives.

My hope is that through considering the power of charm in politics, we will also better understand its significance in everyday life. As we increasingly brand ourselves on social media, some of the methods of political charm and charm offensives shape our everyday lives as well. Understanding these techniques could help us better navigate our offline and online personalities in these confusing, ever-shifting, but occasionally hopeful times. Realizing the frequent similarities between how charm operates in personal and public lives will also make us see that charm is a crucial feature of our existence and will directly shape our democratic future.

NOTES ON METHODS

Chapter 2

LIBERAL CHARM: NEW ZEALAND PRIME MINISTER JACINDA ARDERN

For the analysis of Jacinda Ardern's official Facebook account, 111 posts that were published between July 2017 and June 2021 were taken into consideration. Posts were selected according to popularity, as they had to reach at least twenty thousand likes before February 2021. Focus was also laid on time periods like the initial outbreak of the coronavirus disease in New Zealand. In February and March 2021, for two months all posts were captured to get a fuller picture of everything published and the variance of feedback. To arrive at a nuanced understanding of events of national and international importance such as the terrorist attacks in Christchurch in March 2019, information was drawn from international legacy media sources (BBC, the *Guardian*, etc.) as well as New Zealand's government announcements. Visual information (e.g., Ardern's outfits) was saved in screenshots from Facebook. Statistical data on general social media use in New Zealand was drawn from Statista and yearly reports by social media marketing agency Mosh. New School for Social Research PhD student Olivia Steiert contributed to the analysis as a research assistant.

Chapter 3

ILLIBERAL CHARM: HUNGARIAN PRIME MINISTER VIKTOR ORBÁN

Eötvös Loránd University (Budapest) PhD candidate Veronika Kövesdi and I closely analyzed Orbán's Facebook posts from April 3, 2021, until April 3, 2022. A total of 793 individual posts were uploaded to Orbán's Facebook account during the analyzed time. This includes visual and textual content, video, and live video posts, as well as profile or cover image changes. For the selected posts, we made no distinction between photo and video content. The median number of likes was 14,245. As we were primarily interested in the strategic construction of Orbán's magnetic personality, we focused on posts that had resonated most with his audiences. We regarded posts that received more than twenty thousand likes as "popular." A total of 226 posts reached this threshold. In an initial round of interpreting Orbán's Facebook feed, we defined a set of categories that seemed to capture recurring themes such as Hungarian tradition, religion, references to history, and the staging of Orbán as simultaneously a relatable figure in domestic contexts and a powerful figure on the global stage. We then identified five main themes in the corpus: dominance, drawing the nation's boundaries, presence, gentleness, and political competence. The revised categories and their characteristics were documented in a codebook. In addition to highlighting the general characteristics of each category, we also selected images for close reading to show the most representative examples.

Kövesdi and I both resided in Budapest during most of the time of analysis, interacting in a space marked by Orbán's communication across many channels. In addition to watching television, listening to radio, and following relevant online media platforms, we had the opportunity to observe Orbán's offline communication as well, such as billboards and posters that appeared regularly on the streets of Budapest. Our thinking was shaped by conversations in Hungary, both academic and "everyday." Some of the research resulted in a journal article: Sonnevend and Kövesdi (2023) (the article includes an abridged version of the codebook as an appendix). The Orbán chapter in this book includes further, newer empirical examples that were posted to his Facebook's account after our initial journal article's publication. The chapter also builds on my peer-reviewed journal article Sonnevend (2024) about Orbán as a political "celebrity" on the global stage.

Chapter 4

CHARM OFFENSIVE IN DIPLOMACY: IRANIAN FOREIGN MINISTER MOHAMMAD JAVAD ZARIF

With University of Michigan PhD candidate Yuval Katz, I performed visual and textual analysis of the negotiations' journalistic coverage in the Israeli and American press from March 1 to March 31, 2015. We analyzed ninety-five articles that discussed the deal, collected from four media outlets: the American *New York Times* (*NYT*) and *Wall Street Journal* (*WSJ*) and the Israeli *Haaretz* and *Israel Hayom*. In order to put the negotiations in comparative perspective, we also did textual analysis of eighty-eight articles from the same outlets covering Netanyahu's speech and his attempts at reelection. Outlets were chosen in order to represent a variety of political opinions, as two of them are considered liberal (*NYT* and *Haaretz*) and two conservative (*WSJ* and *Israel Hayom*). We decided to focus on mainstream press coverage as these news outlets are highly influential in shaping public opinion and policy making in the analyzed countries.

Articles were located using the search terms "Iran" and "nuclear" in the internal search engine on the four news sites, complemented by Google's advanced search option. We focused on articles that discussed the personality of Zarif, his impression management, the personal relationships he forged, and the effect he had on other people through his affective political style. The rest of the corpus was used to situate the flow of the events in their respective political contexts.

Textual analysis, which reflects on rhetorical strategies employed during a charm offensive, was complemented with a visual analysis that reveals how relationships and intimacy are created in this process. We performed quantitative and qualitative content analysis of Zarif's photos that appeared on three popular Israeli news sources (*Haaretz*, *Ynet* and *Israel Hayom*) and three American news sources (*NYT*, *Washington Post*, and *WSJ*) during March 2015. A codebook was constructed, containing questions focusing on the number of people with whom Zarif interacted, their identity, the power relations apparent in the photo, the type of relationship forged between Zarif and others, the scene captured by the photo, and Zarif's use of body language—particularly conciliatory and amicable gestures like smiles.

Overall, forty-eight photos of Zarif were analyzed; they were complemented by 118 photos of Netanyahu, also from March 2015, to provide a larger visual context for analysis. Coding was done in three rounds by two independent coders, until reaching an intercoder reliability score of at least 0.7 for each question based on Cohen's kappa test.[1] Photos were then recoded by a third, independent coder. We supplemented the results with a close reading of the photos.

We published some of the results in a peer-reviewed journal article: Sonnevend and Katz (2020) (the article includes the codebook as an appendix). Youngrim Kim (University of Michigan) and Anna Blumberg (the New School for Social Research) contributed to the analysis as research assistants.

Chapter 5

UNEXPECTED CHARM: NORTH KOREAN LEADER KIM JONG-UN

With University of Michigan PhD candidate Youngrim Kim, I examined Kim Jong-un's charm offensive as covered by the American and South Korean press from Kim's New Year's Day address on January 1, 2018, until his meeting with the US president on June 12, 2018. Through thematic analysis of the press coverage, we tracked the North Korean leader's steps toward shifting his own and his country's image, and we analyzed how American and South Korean journalists chose to depict these steps.

To investigate how North Korea's diplomatic maneuvers were mediated, we focused on the journalistic coverage of North Korea and Kim Jong-un in the American and the South Korean press from January 1 to June 30, 2018. January 1, 2018 was selected as the starting date because Kim Jong-un's New Year's Day address was the point when the international media began to pay attention to North Korea's changing diplomacy. We examined articles that were published until June 30 to include the coverage of the Trump-Kim summit. Articles were collected from three American and two South Korean media outlets: the *New York Times*, the *Washington Post*, the *Wall Street Journal*, *Chosun*, and *Hankyoreh*. These newspapers were chosen to represent diverse political opinions; three of them tend to be favored by liberals (*NYT*, the *Washington Post*, and *Hankyoreh*), whereas the other two cater more to conservatives (*WSJ* and *Chosun*). Articles were located using the search terms "North Korea" (북한) and "charm" (매력), "appease" (유화), "peace offensive" (평화 공세), and "image" (이미지) in the internal search engines of the news websites. This search resulted in eighty-four articles in the American and 136 articles in the South Korean press. We examined news articles to compare the different vocabulary, tones, and meanings that are implied by American and South Korean journalists. After a close reading of the articles, we conducted a thematic analysis and identified repetitive themes in the media coverage of Kim's charm offensive. We offered a three-part analysis of the data. First, we provided descriptive information about how many times the term "charm offensive" was mentioned in the American and South Korean newspapers and whether journalists used alternative concepts and vocabularies to describe the same phenomenon. Such a difference in frequency was then interpreted in relation to each country's sociocultural context and historical relationship with North Korea. Also, to examine the chronological progression of the term in association with North Korea, we counted the number of times "charm offensive" was mentioned in the American news coverage of North Korea from 2000 to 2018. Then we examined the main strategies that Kim Jong-un used to run his charm offensive to successfully prompt a reformulation of foreign audiences' perception of North Korea. We analyzed these strategies based on how the international media recalibrated its image of North Korea from "unpredictable threat" to "legitimate partner" in international diplomacy. By looking at both the American and the South Korean press, we attempted to find similar representations of the charm offensive that traveled transnationally. Finally, we also examined how Kim's charm offensive was received by the American and the South Korean press by analyzing the journalistic attitudes expressed in the articles. We published some of the findings in a peer-reviewed journal article: Sonnevend and Kim (2020).

Chapter 6

AUTHENTICITY WITHOUT CHARM: GERMAN CHANCELLOR ANGELA MERKEL

New School for Social Research Sociology PhD student Olivia Steiert and I analyzed a total of 2,023 posts from 2015 until 2021 on Angela Merkel's Instagram account @ bundeskanzlerin (renamed as @bundeskanzlerinMerkel from November 2021 onward). We tentatively identified three strategic phases in style and content as we sorted the material. We outlined an initial experimental phase (June 2015 to December 2016), a consolidation phase (January 2017 to March 2020) and a crisis communication phase (March 2020 to November 2021) based on apparent changes in visual representational strategies. Next, fifty posts were selected randomly for each phase to get a representative sample and allow for a more systematic tracking. For videos, screenshots functioned as static visuals. For slideshows, only the cover image was taken into consideration. The 150 posts were then coded for their level of individualization and their contribution to aspects of "mediated authenticity"— as translated into visuality. To get a sense of how strongly Merkel as a person (rather than as an officeholder, as leader of her party, or as the government as a whole) was visually at the center of the account, the visuals were scanned for four categories of visual personalization: (1a) Is Merkel depicted?

(1b) Is she alone? (2a) If 1a, do we see her face? (2b) Does she display any emotion?

Photos that showed Merkel were also coded for a depiction of a frontstage or backstage environment and a formal versus intimate atmosphere. A backstage visual would show Merkel in surroundings that citizens usually do not have access to. A visual with an "informal" and perhaps intimate atmosphere would show Merkel in conversation with her staff, doing reading, or traveling seemingly by herself. To get an insight into the depiction of Merkel vis-à-vis other heads of state and their own claims to authenticity, ten visuals depicting her with political leaders were analyzed for relational aspects: Is she depicted as smaller or bigger or on an eye level with them? Does she dominate the interaction or take up the center of the composition? Does she touch or is she being touched by her interlocutor? These visual aspects were drawn from previous studies analyzing Merkel's presentation as gendered.[2] To illustrate the insights drawn from this data set more clearly, in the last step three exemplary visuals from each phase were selected to be discussed in more depth and with more extensive context.

Parts of this research resulted in a peer-reviewed journal article: Sonnevend and Steiert (2022).

For further methodological details please consult the published peer-reviewed journal articles.

ACKNOWLEDGMENTS

There are so many to acknowledge that I am worried I will leave out somebody!

I am particularly thankful for the opportunity to present my early book proposal draft at the New York University Sociology of Culture Workshop on April 11, 2019. Paul DiMaggio believed in the project even when it was just a vague draft. He recommended it to Princeton University Press—a testament to his creative, open, and interdisciplinary thinking. At Princeton, sociology editor Meagan Levinson was much more than an editor: a wonderful ally in thinking together. After she left Princeton University Press, I had the pleasure to work with Eric Crahan and Rachael Levay, who thoughtfully and professionally ushered through the manuscript. I also would like to thank Erik Beranek and Theresa Liu, who worked very hard on the production aspects of publication, and Kathleen Kageff for her great copyedits. A special thanks goes to the anonymous peer reviewers who provided crucial guidance.

A continuous inspiration came from conversations and email exchanges with Hungarian intellectual, former director of Magvető Publishing House, and mentor extraordinaire Géza Morcsányi, who never let me off the hook. Whenever I would have taken a break, an inspiring and probing email arrived either from him or from his amazing wife, Judit

Balog. Géza passed away in January 2023, and I feel this loss every day.

I have presented the book's chapters in various iterations in many parts of the world. Here I would like to mention two workshops that were real turning points. In April 2018, I visited the Sociological Working Group on Aesthetics, Meaning, and Power (SWAMP) at the Sociology Department of the University of Virginia. I presented an early draft of the book proposal and a related journal article. The extensive discussion at the workshop and further conversations with Isaac Reed, Fiona Greenland, Jeffrey C. Olick, Elisabeth Becker, Christopher Ali, and the great sociology graduate students filled me with inspiration and ideas. Another turning point came in December 2019, when I visited the Communication Department at the University of Haifa following on the invitation of Sharon Ringel. At Haifa an amazing group of qualitative and quantitative researchers asked me the right questions and inspired me to do further research. Then the pandemic hit, and it hit New York very hard. With my family, I left our home in New York City, first for upstate New York, and later, for a year, we made our home in Princeton. These "lonely" months, when conversations mostly turned online and travel became impossible, were formative as I really immersed myself in the manuscript whenever I was not taking care of our toddler or worrying immensely about the state of the world.

Special thanks goes to my New School mentor Robin Wagner-Pacifici, whose own work on anticharisma is a must-read, and to Barbie Zelizer, who has guided me with thoughtful and strategic advice from the moment I decided to write a book about charm. Presentations at the International Communication Association's annual conventions in Fukuoka, San Diego, Prague, Washington, Paris, and Toronto and American Sociological Association presentations in Philadelphia and New York also shaped my thinking. I am thankful for a series of invited talks, including at Yale Law School, the McCormack Graduate School of Policy and Global Studies at the University of Massachusetts, Central European University, and the University of Leeds.

The book's Orbán chapter would not have been possible without the generous institutional support of the Democracy Institute at Central European University in Budapest, where I spent the sabbatical year of 2021–22. I particularly want to thank László Bruszt for his warm and supportive welcome. I loved the community of the Wallenberg Guesthouse in the beautiful castle area of Budapest, where I made progress on the manuscript, while our child attended the excellent Hungarian Montessori day care Bilimbó.

Media interviews can also help sharpen a book's argument and communicate the findings to broader publics. I am particularly thankful for the opportunity to give an extensive interview about my work and life in the popular *Friderikusz* video podcast in July 2022 (available on YouTube with English subtitles). The reporter's probing and thoughtful questions particularly shaped the conclusion of this book. My author photograph was taken on this occasion by photographer Kornél Kocsány.

I had great New School for Social Research doctoral students as research assistants throughout the book's research and writing: Marijn Nura Mado, Anna Blumberg, Ágnes Szanyi, and Khaled Alsenan. I particularly want to thank Olivia Steiert and Adam Koehler Brown for their dedicated and brilliant work in the final stages of completion. And a big thank-you goes to my doctoral, master's, and undergraduate students in my New School seminars, whose commentary directly shaped this manuscript as it went through multiple iterations.

I built on content from the following peer-reviewed journal articles I cowrote with doctoral students: Sonnevend and Katz (2020); Sonnevend and Kim (2020); Sonnevend and Steiert (2022); and Sonnevend and Kövesdi (2023).

I fondly recall conversations about the project over the years with Elihu and Ruth Katz, Monroe E. Price, Aimée Brown Price, Paddy Scannell, Sarah-Banet Weiser, Aswin Punathambekar, Zohar Kampf, Meital Balmas, Paul Frosh, Gunn Enli, Simon Lübke, Rivka Ribak, Susan Douglas, Jeffrey Goldfarb, Eszter Hargittai, Eszter Zimányi, István Deák, Péter György, Jeffrey C. Alexander, Richard Kessler, Simon Monette, Gina Neff, Ri Pierce-Grove, Rasmus Kleis Nielsen, Sharon Ringel, Nadia Kaneva, Hesna Al Ghaoui, Jack M. Balkin, Antigoné Dellagrammatika, Dávid Lafka, Sid Bedingfield, Valerie Belair-Gagnon, Colin Agur, Limor Shifman, Ben Peters, John Durham Peters, Daniel Kreiss, András Metzinger, Ildikó Magyari, Rachel Sherman, Elzbieta Matynia, Jim Miller, Virág Molnár, Ignacia M. Eschelbach, Mari Györgyey, Veronika Pistyur, Péter Kondor, Zsófia Bán, Katalin Orbán, Motti Neiger, András Bozóki, Katalin Kovács, and the Sonnevend and Schudson families, among others. Special thanks goes to my father, Péter Sonnevend, who regularly sent me international literature about charm and supported me in every possible way.

Finally, I would like to thank Michael Schudson, my husband, and Noah Peter Schudson, our son, for their endless charm and love. They provided daily empirical material for this book. Michael has been a true cheerleader, regularly reminding me of this book's importance, in the most charming ways. When thinking about our political future, I continuously had our little Noah in my mind. He will navigate a world marked by seductive and deceptive political personalities, climate change, global pandemics, political extremism, and a dreadful desire for eliminating nuance and empathy in online worlds. It is my sincere hope that he will find his way to happiness and balance as he builds his ark and navigates these waters. All mention of superheroes in this book is for him.

NOTES

Introduction

1. Alexander, Giesen, and Mast, 2006; Moffitt, 2016.
2. Balmas and Sheafer, 2013; Downey and Stanyer, 2010; Van Aelst, Sheafer, and Stanyer, 2012.
3. Weber, 1968, 241.
4. Krogstad and Storvik, 2006.
5. Chalaby, 2002, 154.
6. Papacharissi, 2019.
7. Alexander, Giesen, and Mast, 2006.
8. Sonnevend, 2019.

1. *Charm*

1. Long and Graesser, 1988, 37.
2. Sauder, 2020.
3. Brown, 2010, 26.
4. Weber, 1968.
5. *Clarion Ledger*, November 2, 2008, cited in Bligh and Kohles, 2009, 484.
6. Alexander, 2006.
7. Beyer, 1999; Eisenstadt and Weber, 1968; Sheafer, 2001; Shils, 1965.
8. McNeil, 2021.
9. Holladay and Coombs, 1994; Tracy and Arden, 2006; Cabane, 2012.
10. Scannell, 2014, 29–32.
11. Hearn, 2008; Banet-Weiser, 2012.
12. Marcus, 2019.
13. McGregor, 2018.
14. Yang et al., 2008.
15. Balmas, 2019.
16. Hund, 2023, 1.
17. Casullo and Colalongo, 2022.
18. Banet-Weiser, 2012; Enli, 2015; Lübke, 2021; Hund, 2023.
19. Alexander, 2006; Alexander, 2010; Greenberg, 2016.
20. Papacharissi, 2021, 117.

21. Einenkel, 2017.

22. Goodman, 2016.

23. Ekberg, 2016.

24. Dumitrica, 2014.

25. Langer, 2011; Dumitrica and Gaden, 2015.

26. Guy, 2023.

27. Sorensen, 2021.

28. Cramer, 2016, 34.

29. Mudde and Rovira Kaltwasser, 2017; Moffitt, 2016; Mendonça and Caetano, 2021; Jagers and Walgrave, 2007.

30. Sonnevend and Kövesdi, 2023; Farkas and Bene, 2022.

31. Dean, 2014.

32. Rai, 2019.

33. Carreira da Silva and Rogenhofer, 2023.

34. Papacharissi, 2015; see also Papacharissi, 2021.

35. Kreiss, 2018; Sonnevend, 2018.

36. Dumitrica and Gaden, 2015.

37. Shivaram and Schneider, 2022.

38. Place, 2021.

39. AFP, 2017.

40. Wagner-Pacifici, 2017, 1.

41. Boorstin, (1962) 1987.

42. Boorstin, 1987, 57.

43. Dayan and Katz, 1992.

44. Repnikova, 2018.

45. Ardern, 2021a.

46. Enli, 2015, 1.

47. Biden, 2021.

48. Müller, 2016.

49. Mudde, 2004, 543.

50. Diderot, 1957, 34.

51. Peters, 1993; Giesen, 2012.

52. Silverman, 2023.

53. Goldthwaite Young, 2023, 11.

54. Kreiss, Lawrence, and McGregor, 2020, 3.

55. Obama, 2018, 236.

56. Pressler, 2017; see also Sutton, 2007; Sutton, 2010; Sutton, 2017.

57. Hoffer, 1994.

58. Kreiss, 2012; Dumitrica and Gaden, 2015; Enli, 2017.

59. Nielsen and Ganter, 2022.

60. Hund, 2023.

61. Horton and Wohl, 1956, 215.

62. McGregor, 2018; Farkas et al., 2022; Muñoz and Towner, 2017; Poulakidakos and Giannouli, 2019; Steffan, 2020.

63. Dumitrica, 2014; John, 2017.

64. Lawrence et al., 2016; McGregor, Lawrence, and Cardona, 2017.

65. McGregor, 2018, 1152.

66. Nielsen, 2012; Chadwick, 2013; Craig, 2016; Enli and Syvertsen, 2016.

67. De Vreese et al., 2018.

68. Sonnevend, 2019.

69. Nye, 2004; Kampf, 2016; Kurlantzick, 2007; Akbarzadeh, 2009.

70. Aronczyk, 2013.

71. Nye, 1990; Nye, 2004.

72. Nye, 2004, 11.

73. Nye, 2004, 7.

74. *Fresno Bee* Archive, 1956, 6.

75. *New York Times*, 1956.

76. Cull, 2019, 17.

77. Zhang and Benoit, 2004.

78. Manor, 2019.

79. Golan, 2013.

80. Papacharissi, 2015.

2. Liberal Charm

1. Taub, 2023.

2. Ardern, 2021c.

3. Ardern, 2018b.

4. Ardern, 2021a.

5. Ardern, 2018a.

6. *Contrasting Styles*, 2018.

7. Ardern, 2019.

8. Ardern, 2021d.

9. Ardern, 2021e.

10. Ardern, 2021f.

11. Ardern, 2020.

12. Cullinane, 2018.

13. Ardern, 2021g.

14. Ardern, 2021h.

15. Sandberg, 2018.

16. Khan, 2019.

17. Women in the World, 2019.

18. J. Kim, 2019.

19. Bittner, 2023.

20. Crowe, 2019.

21. Banet-Weiser, 2018.

3. Illiberal Charm

1. Walker, 2018.
2. *The Times*, 2011.
3. Lendvai, 2018.
4. Walker, 2018.
5. Metz and Plesz, 2022; Szelényi, 2023.
6. Metz and Oross, 2019.
7. Körösényi, 2006.
8. Hlousek, 2015; Metz and Oross, 2019.
9. Rényi, 2021.
10. Rényi and Herczeg, 2022.
11. Gerő and Sik, 2020, 39.
12. Szabó, 2022.
13. In July 2023, Twitter was rebranded to "X."
14. Ben-Ghiat, 2020.
15. Rényi, 2021.
16. Orbán, 2021c.
17. Müller, 2016, 3.
18. Finchelstein, 2024.
19. Orbán, 2021b.
20. Farkas and Bene, 2022.
21. Jobbik is a right-wing party that was in coalition with left liberals to beat Orbán in the elections in 2022.
22. Orbán, 2021a.
23. Casullo and Colalongo, 2022, 63.
24. Alexander, 2008, 782.
25. Levi-Strauss, 1955; Barthes, 1974; Sonnevend, 2016.

4. Charm Offensive in Diplomacy

1. Reuters, 2015.
2. Heimann and Kampf, 2021; Kampf et al., 2021.
3. Bahgat, 2006; Izadi and Saghaye-Biria, 2007.
4. Zarif, 2014, 49.
5. *Washington Post* Staff, 2015.
6. Ravid, 2015.
7. Eqbali and Fitch, 2015.
8. Baker, 2015.
9. Solomon and Norman, 2015b.
10. Wright, 2015.
11. Norman and Schwartz, 2015.
12. Gordon, 2015b.

13. Sanger, 2015.
14. Gordon, 2015a.
15. Solomon and Norman, 2015a.
16. E.g., Alster, 2019; Schneider, 2013.
17. Georgy, 2019.
18. *Haaretz*, 2015.
19. Sanger, 2015.
20. Erdbrink, 2015.
21. Alexander, 2006, 32.

5. Unexpected Charm

1. Rich, 2018, para. 8.
2. Cohen and Liptak, 2018.
3. Chung, 2012; Jeong and Shin, 2015.
4. Jeong and Shin, 2015.
5. Jeong and Shin, 2015.
6. Suh and Yoo, 1997.
7. Suh and Yoo, 1997.
8. Jeong and Shin, 2015.
9. Chun, 2009; Jeong and Shin, 2015.
10. Jae-Hoon Lee, 2018.
11. Oh, 2018.
12. Choe, 2018b, para. 18.
13. *Wall Street Journal* Editorial Board, 2018, para. 9.
14. Fifield, 2018b, para. 13.
15. Ives and McDermid, 2018, para. 6.
16. Rich and Choe, 2018, para. 4.
17. Choe, 2018b, para. 18.
18. S.-M. Lee, 2018, para. 3.
19. M. Kim, 2018, para. 1.
20. Friedman, 2018.
21. Bae, 2018.
22. Landler, 2018, para. 19.
23. *New York Times* Editorial Board, 2018, para. 7.
24. Jin, 2018, para. 5.
25. S.-M. Chang, 2018, para. 1.
26. Rich, 2018, paras. 17–18.
27. Cho, 2018, para. 2.
28. Choe, 2018a, para. 24.
29. Choe, 2018c, paras. 3–12.
30. J.-Y. Ahn, 2018.
31. Y.-H. Kim, 2018, para. 2.

32. S. Kim, 2018, para. 12.

33. S.-Y. Ahn, 2018, para. 3.

34. Noh and Seong, 2018; Soo-Hyun Park, 2018.

35. Choe, 2018c, para. 19.

36. Fifield, 2018a, para. 5.

37. Parker and Fifield, 2018, para. 16.

38. Lim, 2018, para. 8.

39. Donati and Dapena, 2018.

40. Rich, 2018, para. 14.

41. Ignatius, 2018; Lyons, 2018.

42. Kang, 2018.

43. Yoo, 2018.

44. Cho, 2018, para. 2.

45. Lim, 2018, para. 1.

46. Han, 2018; Yoon, 2018.

47. Kim, Y.-C., 2018, para. 4.

48. Lee, J.-S., 2018, para. 1.

49. Noh and Seong, 2018, para. 3.

50. Y.-H. Chang, 2018, para. 2.

51. Joo-Hyun Lee, 2018, para. 4.

52. Sun-Ha Park, 2018, para. 6.

53. *Wall Street Journal* Editorial Board, 2018, paras. 1–5.

54. Mead, 2018, para. 1.

55. Tharoor, 2018, para. 3.

56. Choe, 2018a, para. 20.

57. Rich and Choe, 2018, para. 25.

58. Choe, 2018a, para. 5.

59. Perlez, 2018, para. 4.

60. Fifield, 2018a, para. 2.

61. Myers and Choe, 2018, para. 2.

62. Fifield, 2018a, para. 8.

63. Lyons, 2018, para. 8.

64. Choe, 2018b, para. 8.

65. Kang, 2018, para. 4.

66. I.-H. Lee, 2018, para. 7.

67. Eberstadt, 2018, paras. 1–2.

68. Cho, 2018, para. 2.

69. K.-M. Park, 2018, para. 3.

70. Malcolm, 2018.

6. Authenticity without Charm

1. *ZDF Politbarometer*, n.d.
2. Bennhold, 2021.
3. Sauerbrey, 2021; Morris, 2021.
4. Tworek, Beacock, and Ojo, 2020.
5. Kinnebrock and Knieper, 2014.
6. Grothaus, 2018; Joosse, 2018.
7. Lünenborg and Maier, 2015.
8. Lünenborg and Maier, 2015.
9. Mendonça and Caetano, 2021; McGuire et al., 2020; Jones, 2021; Blasch, 2021; Bene, 2017.
10. Wagner-Pacifici, 2023.

7. The Power of Charm in Global Politics

1. Joosse and Zelinsky, 2023.
2. Hersh, 1997, 14, emphasis added.
3. Bloland, 2000; Maté and Maté, 2022.
4. See Bryant, 2020.
5. Young, 2016.
6. Sonnevend and Steiert, 2022; Wagner-Pacifici, 2023.
7. Canovan, 1999.
8. Bittner, 2023.
9. Trump, 2020, 5.
10. Banet-Weiser and Higgins, 2023.
11. Ellen Spira Hattenbach at the private memorial service for Marvin Spira on January 30, 2021.

Notes on Methods

1. Lombard, Snyder-Duch, and Bracken, 2002.
2. Koch and Holtz-Bacha, 2008; Lünenborg and Maier, 2015; Mushaben, 2018.

BIBLIOGRAPHY

AFP. 2017. "Beach Stroll by Modi, Netanyahu Makes Internet Waves." *Times of Israel*, July 6. https://www.timesofisrael.com/beach-stroll-by-modi-netanyahu -causes-internet-waves/.

Ahn, J.-Y. 2018. "'Puk Chŏngsanggukkaro Karyŏ Pyŏnhwa T'Aek'Ae' 'uriga Puge Chunŭn Kŏnman Kadŭk.'" *Chosun*, April 28.

Ahn, So-Young. 2018. "Hyŏnsongwŏrŭi 'hyŏpsang Imija Chŏllyŏk' 2015nyŏn Chun-gguk Ttaewanŭn Tallatta." *Chosun*, January 15. https://news.chosun.com/site /data/html_dir/2018/01/15/2018011502361.html.

Akbarzadeh, Shahram. 2009. "Obama and the US Policy Change on Iran." *Global Change, Peace and Security* 21, no. 3:397–401.

Alexander, Jeffrey C. 2006. "Cultural Pragmatics: Social Performance between Ritual and Strategy." In *Social Performance: Symbolic Action, Cultural Pragmatics, and Ritual*, 29–90. Cambridge: Cambridge University Press.

———. 2008. "Iconic Consciousness: The Material Feeling of Meaning." *Environment and Planning D: Society and Space* 26, no. 5:782–94.

———. 2010. *The Performance of Politics: Obama's Victory and the Democratic Struggle for Power.* New York: Oxford University Press.

Alexander, Jeffrey C., Bernhard Giesen, and Jason L. Mast. 2006. *Social Performance: Symbolic Action, Cultural Pragmatics, and Ritual.* Cambridge Cultural Social Studies. Cambridge: Cambridge University Press.

Alster, Guy. 2019. "The Fall of the Architect of the Nuclear Deal Is a Bad Sign from Iran." *Walla News*, February 26. https://news.walla.co.il/item/3221101.

Ardern, Jacinda. 2018a. "UN Speech." Iowa State University: Archives of Women's Political Communication, September 27. https://awpc.cattcenter.iastate.edu /2019/04/18/un-speech-september-27-2018/.

Ardern, Jacinda. 2018b. "As We Head Home." *Facebook*, June 23. https://www .facebook.com/45300632440/videos/10155333604817441.

Ardern, Jacinda. 2019. "One of New Zealand's Darkest Days." *Guardian*, March 15. https://www.theguardian.com/world/2019/mar/15/one-of-new-zealands -darkest-days-jacinda-ardern-responds-to-christchurch-shooting.

Ardern, Jacinda. 2020. "Call with Joe Biden." *Facebook*, November 23. https://www .facebook.com/45300632440/videos/420479955990081/.

Ardern, Jacinda. 2021a. "I Was Meant to Do a Facebook Live Tonight but I Left It Too Late." *Facebook*, November 22. https://www.facebook.com/jacindaardern /photos/a.10151319297407441/10158242482402441/?type=3.

Ardern, Jacinda. 2021b. "What's Our Job in Parliament?" *Facebook*, April 14. https://www.facebook.com/jacindaardern/posts/pfbid0HLua2JYAnAyNu6 WnUvRcrcSDDnzpKVBFcR62R9uaGwLCKseTRUmVoQ9cVffS2V5cl.

Ardern, Jacinda. 2021c. "Today We Launched a Housing Package." *Facebook*, March 23. https://www.facebook.com/jacindaardern/videos/4479889732 03270.

Ardern, Jacinda. 2021d. "We Are One." *Beehive*, March 13. https://www.beehive .govt.nz/speech/speech-ko-t%C4%81tou-t%C4%81tou-%E2%80%93-we-are -one-national-remembrance-service-march-15-mosque-attack.

Ardern, Jacinda. 2021e. "Thought You Might Want to Join Us." *Facebook*, January 31. https://www.facebook.com/jacindaardern/videos/533512604717419.

Ardern, Jacinda. 2021f. "Good Morning." *Facebook*, February 5. https://www .facebook.com/jacindaardern/videos/529733868001462.

Ardern, Jacinda. 2021g. "Going through Letters." *Facebook*, March 6. https:// www.facebook.com/jacindaardern/photos/a.10151312135452441/101577237 70682441/.

Ardern, Jacinda. 2021h. "COVID-19 Vaccine Rollout." *Facebook*, February 11. https://www.facebook.com/jacindaardern/videos/247332813558373.

Aronczyk, Melissa. 2013. *Branding the Nation: The Global Business of National Identity*. Oxford: Oxford University Press.

Bae, Yong-Jin. 2018. "Puk'an Inmin Moksum Tugo Mohŏmhaesŏn an Toenda." *Chosun*, May 13. http://news.chosun.com/site/data/html_dir/2018/05/11 /2018051101591.html.

Bahgat, Gawdat. 2006. "Nuclear Proliferation: The Islamic Republic of Iran." *Iranian Studies* 39, no. 3:307–27.

Baker, Peter. 2015. "G.O.P. Senators' Letter to Iran about Nuclear Deal Angers White House." *New York Times*, March 9. https://www.nytimes.com/2015/03 /10/world/asia/white-house-faults-gop-senators-letter-to-irans-leaders.html.

Balmas, Meital. 2019. "National Leaders' Personality Cues and Americans' Attitudes toward Their Countries." *International Journal of Public Opinion Research* 31, no. 4:694–713.

Balmas, Meital, and Tamir Sheafer. 2013. "Leaders First, Countries After: Mediated Political Personalization in the International Arena." *Journal of Communication* 63, no. 3:454–75.

Banet-Weiser, Sarah. 2012. *Authentic TM: Politics and Ambivalence in a Brand Culture*. Critical Cultural Communication. New York: New York University Press.

———. 2018. *Empowered: Popular Feminism and Popular Misogyny*. Durham, NC: Duke University Press.

Banet-Weiser, Sarah, and Kathryn Claire Higgins. 2023. *Believability: Sexual Violence, Media, and the Politics of Doubt*. Cambridge: Polity.

Barel, Zvi. 2015. "Commentary: Give Up the Nuclear Program, We Will Give You Assad." *Haaretz*, March 20. https://www.haaretz.co.il/news/world/middle-east/.premium-1.

Barthes, Roland. 1974. *Mythologies*. New York: Hill and Wang.

Bene, Márton. 2017. "Go Viral on the Facebook! Interactions between Candidates and Followers on Facebook during the Hungarian General Election Campaign of 2014." *Information, Communication and Society* 20, no. 4:513–29.

Ben-Ghiat, Ruth. 2020. *Strongmen: Mussolini to the Present*. New York: W. W. Norton.

Bennhold, Katrin. 2021. "Angela Merkel's Parting Message to Germany: Trust One Another." *New York Times*, December 2. https://www.nytimes.com/2021/12/02/world/europe/angela-merkel-farewell-germany.html.

Beyer, Janice M. 1999. "Taming and Promoting Charisma to Change Organizations." *Leadership Quarterly* 10, no. 2:307–30.

Biden, Joseph R., Jr. 2021. "Inaugural Address by President Joseph R. Biden, Jr." *The White House*, January 20. https://www.whitehouse.gov/briefing-room/speeches-remarks/2021/01/20/inaugural-address-by-president-joseph-r-biden-jr/.

Bittner, Vanessa K. 2023. "Dialectic Icons: Controversial Public Figures as Emotional Catalysts in Contentious Political Discourse." *Emotions and Society* 5, no. 3:257–76.

Blasch, Lisa. 2021. "Indexing Authenticity in Visual Political (Social Media) Communication: A Metapragmatics-Based Analysis of Two Visual Registers of the Authentic." *Multimodal Communication* 10, no. 1:37–53.

Bligh, Michelle C., and Jeffrey C. Kohles. 2009. "The Enduring Allure of Charisma: How Barack Obama Won the Historic 2008 Presidential Election." *Leadership Quarterly* 20, no. 3:483–92.

Bligh, Michelle C., and Jill L. Robinson. 2010. "Was Gandhi "Charismatic"? Exploring the Rhetorical Leadership of Mahatma Gandhi." *Leadership Quarterly* 21, no. 5:844–55.

Bloland, Sue Erikson. 2000. "Bill Clinton and John F. Kennedy: The Dark Side of Charisma." *Psychoanalytic Dialogues* 10, no. 2:285–89.

Boczkowski, Pablo J., and Zizi Papacharissi. 2018. *Trump and the Media*. Cambridge, MA: MIT Press.

Boorstin, Daniel J. (1962) 1987. *The Image: A Guide to Pseudo-events in America*. New York: Atheneum.

Brown, Brené. 2010. *The Gifts of Imperfection*. Philadelphia: Hazelden.

Bryant, Lisa. 2020. *Jeffrey Epstein: Filthy Rich*. Netflix.

Cabane, Olivia Fox. 2012. *The Charisma Myth: How Anyone Can Master the Art and Science of Personal Magnetism*. New York: Penguin.

Canovan, Margaret. 1999. "Trust the People! Populism and the Two Faces of Democracy." *Political Studies* 47, no. 1:2–16.

Carreira da Silva, Filipe, and Julius Rogenhofer. 2023. "Populist Things: A Study on the Materiality of Political Ideas." *Sociology Compass* 17, no. 3. https://compass.onlinelibrary.wiley.com/doi/10.1111/soc4.13066.

Casullo, María Esperanza, and Rodolfo E. Colalongo. 2022. "The Populist Body in the Age of Social Media: A Comparative Study of Populist and Non-populist Representation." *Thesis Eleven* 173, no. 1:62–81.

Chadwick, Andrew. 2013. *The Hybrid Media System: Politics and Power*. Oxford Studies in Digital Politics. New York: Oxford University Press.

Chalaby, Jean K. 2002. *The de Gaulle Presidency and the Media: Statism and Public Communications*. New York: Palgrave Macmillan.

Chang, Seong-Min. 2018. "Kimilsŏngŭi Kunsajŏk Kisŭpkwa Kimjŏngŭnŭi Oegyojŏk Yŏksŭp." *Chosun*, April 30. http://news.chosun.com/site/data/html_dir/2018/04/30/2018043000804.html.

Chang, Yong-Hoon. 2018. "Solchik Taedamhan Kimjŏngŭnŭi 'nambuk' 'puk-Mi' Chŏngsanghoedamŭn Kwayŏn Ŏttŏlkka." *Hankyoreh*, March 12. http://www.hani.co.kr/arti/politics/politics_general/835670.html.

Chapman, Madeleine. 2020. *The Most Powerful Woman in the World: How Jacinda Ardern Exemplifies Progressive Leadership*. New York: Skyhorse.

Cho, Eui-Jun. 2018. "T'Ŭrŏmp'Ŭ, Kimjŏngŭnŭi Kyŏmson Hwabŏp Maeryŏk Kongse Taebihae Kwaoebadatta." *Chosun*, June 12. http://news.chosun.com/site/data/html_dir/2018/06/12/2018061200308.html.

Choe, Sang-Hun. 2018a. "Kim Jong-un's Image Shift: From Nuclear Madman to Skillful Leader." *International New York Times*, June 7. https://www.nytimes.com/2018/06/06/world/asia/kim-korea-image.html.

———. 2018b. "Most North Koreans Can't Actually Watch the Olympic Games." *New York Times*, February 15. https://www.nytimes.com/2018/02/15/world/asia/north-korea-olympics-television.html#:~:text=Can%20its%20people%20watch%20them,Korean%20defectors%20in%20the%20South.

———. 2018c. "North Korean Leader, Known for His Bluster, Reveals Diplomatic Skills." *New York Times*, March 7. https://www.nytimes.com/2018/03/07/world/asia/kim-jong-un-north-korea.html.

———. 2018d. "Warm Welcome Home from Olympics for Kim Jong-un's Sister." *International New York Times*, February 12. https://www.nytimes.com/2018/02/12/world/asia/north-korea-kimyo-jong.html.

Chun, Dong-jin. 2009. "Che 1chang Puk'Anŭi Taemi Hyŏpsang Chŏllyakkwa Sŏn'Gun ridŏship—'Pyŏrang Kkŭt Hyŏpsang' Chŏllyakŭl Chungshimŭro." *Unification Strategy* 9, no. 2:9–46.

Chung, Sung-Yoon. 2012. "Puk'an Hwajŏn Yangmyŏn Chŏllyagŭi T'ŭkchinggwa Chŏnmang." *Journal of Strategic Studies* 54, no. 1:65–96.

———. 2014. "Kimjŏngŭn Chŏnggwŏnŭi Taeoegwan'Gyewa Anbojŏllyak: Punsŏk Mit P'Yŏngga Kŭrigo Chŏnmang." *21segi Chŏngch'i Hak'Oebo* 24, no. 1:171–94.

Cohen, Zachary, and Kevin Liptak. 2018. "Trump Praises Kim Jong Un as Honorable, Refuses to Explain Why." *CNN*, April 25. https://www.cnn.com/2018/04/24/politics/trump-kim-jong-un-honorable/index.html.

Contrasting Styles: Trump and Ardern Speak at the UN. 2018. Directed by the *Guardian*.

Craig, Geoffrey. 2016. *Performing Politics: Media Interviews, Debates and Press Conferences.* Contemporary Political Communication. Cambridge, UK: Polity.

Cramer, Katherine J. 2016. *The Politics of Resentment: Rural Consciousness in Wisconsin and the Rise of Scott Walker.* Chicago: University of Chicago Press.

Crowe, David. 2019. "Prime Minister Jacinda Ardern Humbled by Giant Melbourne Mural." *Stuff*, July 19. https://www.stuff.co.nz/national/politics/114383123/prime-minister-jacinda-ardern-humbled-by-giant-melbourne-mural.

Cull, Nicholas J. 2019. *Public Diplomacy: Foundations for Global Engagement in the Digital Age.* Contemporary Political Communication. Cambridge, UK: Polity.

Cullinane, Susannah. 2018. "Pregnant NZ PM Unfazed by 'Sexist' Interview." *CNN Wire Service*, February 26. https://www.cnn.com/2018/02/26/asia/nz-pm-jacinda-ardern-60-minutes/index.html.

Dayan, Daniel, and Elihu Katz. 1992. *Media Events: The Live Broadcasting of History.* Cambridge, MA: Harvard University Press.

Dean, Nelson. 2014. "'Magic' Modi Uses Hologram to Address Dozens of Rallies at Once." *Telegraph*, May 2. https://www.telegraph.co.uk/news/worldnews/asia/india/10803961/Magic-Modi-uses-hologram-to-address-dozens-of-rallies-at-once.html.

Dehghan, Saeed K. 2013. "Mohammad Javad Zarif: Iran's Man on a Diplomatic Mission." *Guardian*, November 25. https://www.theguardian.com/world/2013/nov/25/mohammad-javad-zarif-iran-profile.

de Vreese, C. H., F. Esser, T. Aalberg, C. Reinemann, and J. Stanyer. 2018. "Populism as an Expression of Political Communication Content and Style: A New Perspective." *The International Journal of Press/Politics* 23, no. 4:423–38.

Diderot, Denis. 1957. *The Paradox of Acting.* New York: Hill and Wang.

Donati, Jessica, and Kara Dapena. 2018. "From Name Calling to High Hopes: The Trump-Kim Relationship." *Wall Street Journal*, June 1. https://www.wsj.com/graphics/trump-kim-jong-un-timeline/.

Downey, John, and James Stanyer. 2010. "Comparative Media Analysis: Why Some Fuzzy Thinking Might Help: Applying Fuzzy Set Qualitative Comparative Analysis to the Personalization of Mediated Political Communication." *European Journal of Communication* (London) 25, no. 4:331–47.

Dumitrica, Delia. 2014. "Politics as 'Customer Relations': Social Media and Political Authenticity in the 2010 Municipal Elections in Calgary, Canada." *Javnost* (Ljubljana, Slovenia) 21, no. 1:53–69.

Dumitrica, Delia, and Georgia Gaden. 2015. "The 'Real Deal': Strategic Authenticity, Politics and Social Media." *First Monday* 20, no. 1:30.

Dumont, Theron Q. 2005. *The Art and Science of Personal Magnetism.* New York: Cosimo Classics.

Durkheim, Emile. 1995. *The Elementary Forms of Religious Life.* New York: Free Press.

Eberstadt, Nicholas. 2018. "With Kim Jong Un, There's No 'Win-Win.'" *Wall Street Journal*, May 24. https://www.wsj.com/articles/with-kim-jong-un-theres-no-win-win-1527113196.

Einenkel, Watler. 2017. "That One Time Fox News Attacked President Obama for Asking for Mustard." *Daily Kos*, June 12. https://www.dailykos.com/stories /2017/6/12/1671103/-That-one-time-Fox-News-attacked-President-Obama -for-asking-for-mustard.

Eisenstadt, S., and Max Weber. 1968. *Max Weber on Charisma and Institution Building*. Chicago: University of Chicago Press.

Ekberg, Olaf. 2016. "Photo: Hillary Looks Stunned Touring East Harlem Apartment." *American Mirror*, April 15. https://www.theamericanmirror.com/blog /2016/04/15/photo-hillary-looks-stunned-touring-east-harlem-apartment/.

Enli, Gunn. 2015. *Mediated Authenticity: How the Media Constructs Reality*. New York: Peter Lang.

———. 2017. "Twitter as Arena for the Authentic Outsider: Exploring the Social Media Campaigns of Trump and Clinton in the 2016 US Presidential Election." *European Journal of Communication* (London) 32, no. 1:50–61.

Enli, Gunn, and Trine Syvertsen. 2016. "The End of Television—Again! How TV Is Still Influenced by Cultural Factors in the Age of Digital Intermediaries." *Media and Communication* 4, no. 3:142–53.

Epstein, Joseph, 2018. *Charm: The Elusive Enchantment*. Lanham, MD: Rowman and Littlefield.

Eqbali, Aresu, and Asa Fitch. 2015. "Iran Supreme Leader Criticizes Republican Letter on Nuclear Talks; Ayatollah Ali Khamenei Says GOP Warning Represents 'Collapse in Political Ethics.'" *Wall Street Journal*, March 12. https://www .wsj.com/articles/iran-supreme-leader-criticizes-republican-letter-on-nuclear -talks-1426195767.

Erdbrink, Thomas. 2015. "Iran Hard-Liners Show Restraint on Nuclear Deal." *New York Times*, March 24. https://www.nytimes.com/2015/03/24/world /middleeast/irans-hard-liners-nuclear-talks.html.

Farkas, Xénia, and Márton Bene. 2020. "Images, Politicians, and Social Media: Patterns and Effects of Politicians' Image-Based Political Communication Strategies on Social Media." *International Journal of Press/Politics* 26, no. 1:119–42.

———. 2022. "Orbán Viktor vizuális és verbális populista stílusa a Facebookon." *Politikatudományi Szemle* 31, no. 3:82–108.

Farkas, Xénia, Daniel Jackson, Paweł Baranowski, Márton Bene, Uta Russmann, and Anastasia Veneti. 2022. "Strikingly Similar: Comparing Visual Political Communication of Populist and Non-populist Parties across 28 Countries." *European Journal of Communication* 37, no. 5:545–62.

Fifield, Anna. 2018a. "In a Feel-Good Korea Summit, Kim Lays the Groundwork for Meeting with Trump." *Washington Post*, April 27. https://www.washingtonpost .com/world/asia_pacific/north-and-south-korea-agree-to-work-toward -common-goal-of-denuclearization/2018/04/27/7dcb03d6-4981-11e8-8082 -105a446d19b8_story.html.

———. 2018b. "Photo of Historic Handshake between North and South Korea Goes Viral." *Washington Post*, February 9. https://www.washingtonpost.com

/news/worldviews/wp/2018/02/09/photo-of-historic-handshake-between-north-and-south-korea-goes-viral/.

Finchelstein, Federico. 2024. *The Wannabe Fascists: A Guide to Understanding the Greatest Threat to Democracy*. Oakland: University of California Press.

Fresno Bee Archive. 1956. "General Warns of Critical Years." *Fresno (California) Bee*, September 19. https://fresnobee.newspapers.com/image/702260552/?terms=General%20Warns%20of%20Critical%20Years&match=1.

Friedland, William H. 1964. "For a Sociological Concept of Charisma." *Social Forces* 43, no. 1:18–26.

Friedman, Vanessa. 2018. "The North Korean Cheer Squad Is Playing a Different Olympic Game." *New York Times* (online), February 8. https://www.nytimes.com/2018/02/08/fashion/north-korean-cheer-squad-winter-olympics-2018.html.

Garzia, Diego, Frederico Ferreira da Silva, and Andrea De Angelis. 2022. "Partisan Dealignment and the Personalisation of Politics in West European Parliamentary Democracies, 1961–2018." *West European Politics* 45, no. 2:311–34.

Georgy, Michael. 2019. "Iran's Zarif: Smooth Diplomat Challenged by Hardliners." *Reuters*, February 26. https://www.reuters.com/article/us-iran-zarif-newsmaker-idUSKCN1QE2MI/.

Gerő, Márton, and Endre Sik. 2020. "The Moral Panic Button: Construction and Consequences." In *Europe and the Refugee Response*, edited by Brigitte Suter, Izabella Main, and Elżbieta M. Goździak, 39–58. London: Taylor and Francis.

Giesen, Bernhard. 2012. "Inbetweenness and Ambivalence." In *The Oxford Handbook of Cultural Sociology*, edited by Philip Smith, Ronald N. Jacobs, and Jeffrey C. Alexander, 788–804. New York: Oxford University Press.

Golan, Guy J. 2013. "An Integrated Approach to Public Diplomacy." *American Behavioral Scientist* (Beverly Hills) 57, no. 9:1251–55.

Goldthwaite Young, Dannagal. 2023. *Wrong: How Media, Politics, and Identity Drive Our Appetite for Misinformation*. Baltimore: Johns Hopkins University Press.

Goodman, J. David. 2016. "Hillary Clinton's MetroCard Adventure: Swipe. Wince. Repeat." *New York Times*, April 7. https://www.nytimes.com/2016/04/08/nyregion/hillary-clintons-subway-metrocard-adventure-swipe-wince-repeat.html.

Gordon, Michael R. 2015a. "Kerry Pushes Iran Nuclear Deal Timetable amid Differences with France." *New York Times*, March 21. https://www.nytimes.com/2015/03/22/world/middleeast/kerry-pushes-iran-nuclear-deal-timetable-amid-differences-with-france.html.

———. 2015b. "Kerry Pushing for Agreement in Nuclear Talks." *New York Times*, March 2. https://www.nytimes.com/2015/03/02/world/middleeast/kerry-is-pushing-for-agreement-in-iran-nuclear-talks.html.

Greenberg, David. 2016. *Republic of Spin: An Inside History of the American Presidency*. London: W. W. Norton.

Grothaus, M. 2018. "The Best Reactions to Angela Merkel's Viral Trump G7 Photo." *Fast Company*, June 10. https://www.fastcompany.com/40583410/the-best-reactions-to-angela-merkels-viral-trump-g7-photo.

Guy, Derek. 2023. "3 Expert Shoemakers Say Ron DeSantis Is Probably Wearing Height Boosters." *Politico*, October 31. https://www.politico.com/news/magazine/2023/10/31/desantis-boots-shoemakers-00121044.

Haaretz. 2015. "The Iranian Foreign Minister at the End of Meeting with Kerry in Switzerland: 'We Will Reach an Agreement Eventually.'" *Haaretz*, March 17. https://www.haaretz.co.il/.premium-1.2591622.

Han, Dong-Hee. 2018. "Ch'Ŏlgabang Tŭn Kimjŏngŭn . . . 'chorong' Esŏ 'yumŏ K'Odŭ'ro?" *Chosun*, April 30. https://www.chosun.com/site/data/html_dir/2018/04/30/2018043002093.html.

Hearn, Alison. 2008. "'Meat, Mask, Burden': Probing the Contours of the Branded 'Self.'" *Journal of Consumer Culture* 8, no. 2:197–217.

Heimann, Gadi, and Zohar Kampf. 2021. "What Makes Them Tick: Challenging the Impersonal Ethos in International Relations." *Cooperation and Conflict* 56, no. 3:346–63.

Hersh, Seymour M. 1997. *The Dark Side of Camelot*. Boston: Little, Brown.

Hlousek, Vít. 2015. "Two Types of Presidentialization in the Party Politics of Central Eastern Europe." *Rivista Italiana Di Scienza Politica* 45, no. 3:277–99.

Hoffer, Richard. 1994. "Fatal Attraction?" *Sports Illustrated*, June 27. https://vault.si.com/vault/1994/06/27/fatal-attraction-oj-simpson-stands-accused-of-brutally-killing-two-people-one-of-them-the-woman-he-loved.

Holladay, Sherry J., and W. Timothy Coombs. 1994. "Speaking of Visions and Visions Being Spoken." *Management Communication Quarterly* 8, no. 2:165–89.

Hong, S. 2015. "Kimjŏngŭn Chŏnggwŏnŭi Shindaeoejŏllyak Punsŏk." *Chŏngch'i Chŏngbo Yŏn'Gu* 18, no. 2:59–83.

Horton, Donald, and Richard R. Wohl. 1956. "Mass Communication and Para-social Interaction." *Psychiatry* (Washington, DC) 19, no. 3:215–29.

Hund, Emily. 2023. *The Influencer Industry: The Quest for Authenticity on Social Media*. Princeton, NJ: Princeton University Press.

Ignatius, David. 2018. "Trump Is Wile E. Coyote." *Washington Post*, March 9. https://www.washingtonpost.com/opinions/global-opinions/trump-is-wile-e-coyote/2018/03/08/bc0cac60-2313-11e8-86f6-54bfff693d2b_story.html.

Ives, Mike, and Charles McDermid. 2018. "North Korea, Moscow, Rob Porter: Your Monday Briefing." *New York Times*, February 11. https://www.nytimes.com/2018/02/11/briefing/north-korea-moscow-rob-porter.html.

Izadi, Foad, and Hakimeh Saghaye-Biria. 2007. "A Discourse Analysis of Elite American Newspaper Editorials: The Case of Iran's Nuclear Program." *Journal of Communication Inquiry* 31, no. 2:140–65.

Jagers, Jan, and Stefaan Walgrave. 2007. "Populism as Political Communication Style: An Empirical Study of Political Parties' Discourse in Belgium." *European Journal of Political Research* 46, no. 3:319–45.

Jeong, J., and D. Shin. 2015. "Kimjŏngŭn Shidaeŭi Hwajŏnyangmyŏnjŏnsul Yŏn'Guwa Taeŭngjŏllyak." *Kunsa Yŏn'Gu* 139, no. 1:379–422.

Jin, Jingyi. 2018. "Puk'Aek T'Agyŏrŭi Ch'Ŏnshijiriinhwa." *Hankyoreh*, March 25. http://www.hani.co.kr/arti/opinion/column/837582.html.

John, Nicholas A. 2017. *The Age of Sharing*. Malden, MA: Polity.

Jones, Rodney H. 2021. "The Wounded Leader: The Illness Narratives of Boris Johnson and Donald Trump." *Discourse, Context and Media* 41:100499.

Joosse, Paul. 2018. "Countering Trump: Toward a Theory of Charismatic Counter-roles." *Social Forces* 97, no. 2:921–44.

Joosse, Paul, and Dominik Zelinsky. 2023. "Charismatic Mimicry: Innovation and Imitation in the Case of Volodymyr Zelensky." *Sociological Theory* 41, no. 3:201–28.

Kampf, Zohar. 2016. "Rhetorical Bypasses: Connecting with the Hearts and Minds of People on the Opponent's Side." *Journal of Multicultural Discourses* 11, no. 2: 49–63.

Kampf, Zohar, Dana Chudy, Roni Danziger, and Mia Schreiber. 2021. "'Wait with Falling in Love': Discursive Evaluation of Amicable Messages Conveyed by Opponents." *Journal of Language and Social Psychology* 40, no. 2:188–213.

Kang, In-Sun. 2018. "'Katcha Ollibŭ Kajie Hŭngbunmalla': Mi Chŏnmun'Gadŭl T'Ŭwit'Ŏ Pullatta." *Chosun*, January 4. http://news.chosun.com/site/data /html_dir/2018/01/04/2018010400268.html.

Khan, Sadiq. 2019. "100 Most Influential People 2019: Jacinda Ardern." *Time Magazine*. https://time.com/collection/100-most-influential-people-2019/5567767 /jacinda-ardern/.

Kim, Christine, and Phil Stewart. 2017. "North Korea Says "Breakthrough" Puts U.S. Mainland within Range of Nuclear Weapons." *Reuters*, November 28. https://www.reuters.com/article/uk-northkorea-missiles-report/north-korea -says-breakthrough-puts-u-s-mainland-within-range-of-nuclear-weapons -idUKKBN1DS2J1.

Kim, Jean. 2019. "Jacinda Ardern: The Psychology of an Ideal Woman Leader." *Psychology Today*, April 14. https://www.psychologytoday.com/us/blog/culture -shrink/201904/jacinda-ardern-the-psychology-ideal-woman-leader.

Kim, Mina. 2018. "WP 'Kimyŏjŏngŭn Puk'Anŭi Ibangk'a . . . an'Gugin Maŭm Sarojaba.'" *Hankyoreh*, February 11. http://www.hani.co.kr/arti/international /international_general/831768.html.

Kim, Suki. 2018. "North Korea's Lipstick Diplomacy." *New York Times*, February 9. https://www.nytimes.com/2018/02/08/opinion/north-korea-lipstick -diplomacy.html.

Kim, Yeon-Cheol. 2018. "Kyoryurŭl Turyŏwŏ Mara." *Hankyoreh*, January 14. http:// www.hani.co.kr/arti/opinion/column/827695.html.

Kim, Young-Hee. 2018. "Chŏngŭnssiŭi Maeryŏk Kongserŭl Wae Turyŏwŏhana." *Hankyoreh*, May 3. http://www.hani.co.kr/arti/opinion/column/843173.html.

Kinnebrock, Susanne, and Thomas Knieper. 2014. "Gender and Power Constructions in Visual Political Reporting." *Social and Education History* 3, no. 1:54–77.

Koch, Thomas, and Christina Holtz-Bacha. 2008. "Der Merkel-Faktor - Die Berichterstattung der Printmedien über Merkel und Schröder im Bundestagswahlkampf 2005." In *Frauen, Politik und Medien*, edited by Christina Holtz-Bacha, 49–71. Wiesbaden: VS Verlag für Sozialwissenschaften.

Körösényi, András. 2006. "Mozgékony patthelyzet: Reform és változatlanság között: A politikai és alkotmányos alapszerkezet változásai, 1990–2005." *Politikatudományi Szemle* no. 1:29–68.

Kreiss, Daniel. 2012. *Taking Our Country Back: The Crafting of Networked Politics from Howard Dean to Barack Obama*. Oxford Studies in Digital Politics. New York: Oxford University Press.

———. 2016. "Seizing the Moment: The Presidential Campaigns' Use of Twitter during the 2012 Electoral Cycle." *New Media and Society* 18, no. 8:1473–90.

———. 2018. "The Media Are about Identity, Not Information." In *Trump and the Media*, edited by Zizi Papacharissi and Pablo J. Boczkowski, 93–99. Cambridge, MA: MIT Press.

Kreiss, Daniel, Regina G. Lawrence, and Shannon C. McGregor. 2020. "Political Identity Ownership: Symbolic Contests to Represent Members of the Public." *Social Media and Society* 6, no. 2. https://journals.sagepub.com/doi/full/10.1177/2056305120926495.

Krogstad, Anne, and Aagoth Storvik. 2006. "Seductive Heroes and Ordinary Human Beings: Charismatic Political Leadership in France and Norway." In *Comparative Studies of Social and Political Elites*, edited by Fredrik Engelstad and Trygve Gulbrandsen, 211–45. Leeds: Emerald.

Kurlantzick, Joshua. 2007. *Charm Offensive: How China's Soft Power Is Transforming the World*. Paperback ed. New Republic Books. New Haven, CT: Yale University Press.

Landler, Mark. 2018. "North Korea Asks for Direct Nuclear Talks, and Trump Agrees." *New York Times*, March 8. https://www.nytimes.com/2018/03/08/us/politics/north-korea-kim-jong-un-trump.html.

Langer, Ana. 2011. *The Personalisation of Politics in the UK: Mediated Leadership from Attlee to Cameron*. Manchester: Manchester University Press.

Lawrence, Regina G., Shannon C. McGregor, Arielle Cardona, and Rachel R. Mourão. 2016. "Personalization and Gender: 2014 Gubernatorial Candidates on Social Media." In *Communication and Midterm Elections*, edited by John A. Hendricks and Dan Schill, 191–206. New York: Palgrave Macmillan.

Lee, I.-H. 2018. "Il Kŭgu Ŏllon, 'IOCŭi Nambuk Tanilt'Im Choch'I, Sŭp'Och'Ŭ Kŭnbonŭl Twihŭndŭnŭn Haengwi.'" *Chosun*, January 21. http://news.chosun.com/site/data/html_dir/2018/01/21/2018012100681.html.

Lee, Jae-Hoon. 2018. "Yŏksajŏgin P'Anmunjŏm Sŏnŏn, Kŭ Ŭiminŭn Muŏshin'Ga." *Hankyoreh*, May 4. https://www.hani.co.kr/arti/politics/bluehouse/843326.html.

Lee, Jong-Seok. 2018. "Kŏn'Gunjŏlgwa Kimjŏngŭn: Hojŏnsŏng Tae Shiryongjuŭi." *Hankyoreh*, January 28. http://www.hani.co.kr/arti/opinion/column/829732.html.

Lee, Joo-Hyun. 2018. "3ch'Awŏnŭro Pon Hanbandoŭi Ŏje, Onŭl, Naeil." *Hankyoreh*, April 5. http://www.hani.co.kr/arti/culture/book/839360.html.

Lee, Seon-Mok. 2018. "Oeshin, Ibangk'a Vs Kimyŏjŏng Kudo Chumok . . . P'Yŏngch'Ang Oegyojŏn Sŭngjanŭn Nugu." *Chosun*, February 23. http://news .chosun.com/site/data/html_dir/2018/02/23/2018022302128.html.

Lendvai, Paul. 2018. "'The Most Dangerous Man in the European Union': The Metamorphosis of Viktor Orbán." *Atlantic*, April 7. https://www.theatlantic .com/international/archive/2018/04/viktor-orban-hungary/557246/.

Levi-Strauss, Claude. 1955. "The Structural Study of Myth." *Journal of American Folklore* 68, no. 270:428–44.

Lim, Min-Hyeok. 2018. "Shijinp'Ing Mannarŏ Kago, P'Omp'Eio Purŭgo . . . Kimjŏngŭn G2 Kongnyak." *Chosun*, May 10. http://news.chosun.com/site /data/html_dir/2018/05/10/2018051000305.html.

Lombard, Matthew, Jennifer Snyder-Duch, and Cheryl Campanella Bracken. 2002. "Content Analysis in Mass Communication: Assessment and Reporting of Intercoder Reliability." *Human Communication Research* 28, no. 4:587–604.

Long, Debra L., and Arthur C. Graesser. 1988. "Wit and Humor in Discourse Processing." *Discourse Processes* 11, no. 1:35–60.

Lübke, Simon M. 2021. "Political Authenticity: Conceptualization of a Popular Term." *International Journal of Press / Politics* 26, no. 3:635–53.

Lünenborg, Margreth, and Tanja Maier. 2015. "'Power Politician' or 'Fighting Bureaucrat': Gender and Power in German Political Coverage." *Media, Culture and Society* 37, no. 2:180–96.

Lyons, John. 2018. "From 'Punk Kid' to 21st Century Tyrant: Kim Jong Un Seizes His Moment." *Wall Street Journal: Eastern Edition*, June 8. https://www.wsj .com/articles/from-punk-kid-to-21st-century-tyrant-kim-jong-un-seizes-his -moment-1528467258.

Malcolm, Candice. 2018. "Why Justin Trudeau's India Tour Turned Out to Be a Diplomatic Disaster." *Economic Times*, February 25. https://economictimes .indiatimes.com/news/politics-and-nation/why-justin-trudeaus-india-tour -turned-out-to-be-a-diplomatic-disaster/articleshow/63059621.cms?from =mdr.

Manor, Ilan. 2019. *The Digitalization of Public Diplomacy*. Palgrave Macmillan Series in Global Public Diplomacy. Cham: Springer.

Marcus, Sharon. 2019. *The Drama of Celebrity*. Princeton, NJ: Princeton University Press.

Maté, Gabor, and Daniel Maté. 2022. *The Myth of Normal: Trauma, Illness and Healing in a Toxic Culture*. New York: Penguin.

McGregor, Shannon C. 2018. "Personalization, Social Media, and Voting: Effects of Candidate Self-Personalization on Vote Intention." *New Media and Society* 20, no. 3:1139–60.

McGregor, Shannon C., Regina G. Lawrence, and Arielle Cardona. 2017. "Personalization, Gender, and Social Media: Gubernatorial Candidates' Social Media Strategies." *Information, Communication and Society* 20, no. 2:264–83.

McGuire, David, James E. A. Cunningham, Kae Reynolds, and Gerri Matthews-Smith. 2020. "Beating the Virus: An Examination of the Crisis Communication Approach Taken by New Zealand Prime Minister Jacinda Ardern during the Covid-19 Pandemic." *Human Resource Development International* 23, no. 4:361–79.

McNeil, Liz. 2021. "Monica Lewinsky on Bill Clinton's 'Lethal Charm' and Why She Doesn't Need Anything from Him Anymore." *People Magazine*, September 8. https://people.com/politics/monica-lewinsky-on-bill-clinton-lethal-charm/.

Mead, Walter Russell. 2018. "Kim Yo Jong's Shattered Olympic Dream." *Wall Street Journal: Eastern Edition*, February 13. https://www.wsj.com/articles/kim-yo -jongs-shattered-olympic-dream-1518478897.

Mendonça, Ricardo F., and Renato Duarte Caetano. 2021. "Populism as Parody: The Visual Self-Presentation of Jair Bolsonaro on Instagram." *International Journal of Press / Politics* 26, no. 1:210–35.

Metz, Rudolf, and Dániel Oross. 2019. "Strong Personalities' Impact on Hungarian Party Politics: Viktor Orbán and Gábor Vona." In *Party Leaders in Eastern Europe*, edited by Sergiu Gherghina, 145–70. New York: Springer.

Metz, Rudolf, and Bendegúz Plesz. 2022. *Egy hősre várva: A szavazók populista nézetei és a vezetők karizmája*. Budapest: Társadalomtudományi Kutatóközpont. https://doi.org/10.1177/19401612221100418.

Moffitt, Benjamin. 2016. *The Global Rise of Populism: Performance, Political Style, and Representation*. Stanford, CA: Stanford University Press.

———. 2022. "How Do Populists Visually Represent 'the People'? A Systematic Comparative Visual Content Analysis of Donald Trump and Bernie Sanders' Instagram Accounts." *International Journal of Press / Politics*. 29(1): 74–99. https://journals.sagepub.com/doi/full/10.1177/19401612221100418.

Morris, Loveday. 2021. "After 16 Years, Germany's Merkel Is Stepping Down. Here's How She Built Her Legacy." *Washington Post.com*, September 13. https://www .washingtonpost.com/world/interactive/2021/merkel-germany-legacy/.

Mudde, Cas. 2004. "The Populist Zeitgeist." *Government and Opposition* (London) 39, no. 4:541–63.

Mudde, Cas, and Cristóbal Rovira Kaltwasser. 2017. *Populism: A Very Short Introduction*. New York: Oxford University Press.

Müller, Jan-Werner. 2016. *What Is Populism?* Penguin Politics. Philadelphia: University of Pennsylvania Press.

Muñoz, Caroline Lego, and Terri L. Towner. 2017. "The Image Is the Message: Instagram Marketing and the 2016 Presidential Primary Season." *Journal of Political Marketing* 16, no. 3–4:290–318.

Mushaben, Joyce Marie. 2018. "Kan-Di(E)-Dat? Unpacking Gender Images across Angela Merkel's Four Campaigns for the Chancellorship, 2005–2017." *German Politics and Society* 36, no. 1:31–51.

Myers, Steven Lee, and Choe Sang-Hun. 2018. "What Kim Jong-un May Get in Reaching Out to China." *New York Times* (online), March 27. https://www .nytimes.com/2018/03/27/world/asia/kim-jong-un-china-trip.html.

New York Times. 1956. "Hungarian 'Lift' Near 1,200 Mark." *New York Times*, December 5. https://www.nytimes.com/1956/12/05/archives/hungarian-lift-near-1200-mark-19th-flight-arrives-in-jersey-464.html.

New York Times Editorial Board. 2018. "Donald Trump and North Korea: What a Fine Mess." *New York Times*, March 9. https://www.nytimes.com/2018/03/09/opinion/north-korea-trump.html.

Nielsen, Rasmus Kleis. 2012. *Ground Wars: Personalized Communication in Political Campaigns*. Princeton, NJ: Princeton University Press.

Nielsen, Rasmus Kleis, and Sarah Ganter. 2022. *The Power of Platforms: Shaping Media and Society*. Oxford Studies in Digital Politics. New York: Oxford University Press.

Noh, Ji-Won, and Yeon-Cheol Seong. 2018. "Nodongdangsa Konggae, Risŏlchu Tongban 'Kimjŏngŭnŭi P'Agyŏk' . . . Puk Chŏngsanggukka Pugak." *Hankyoreh*, March 6. http://www.hani.co.kr/arti/politics/defense/834931.html.

Norman, Laurence, and Felicia Schwartz. 2015. "Iran, U.S. Press ahead with Efforts to Seal Nuclear Deal by Month-End; Negotiations Continue as Israeli Leader Benjamin Netanyahu Prepares to Address Congress." *Wall Street Journal: Eastern Edition*, March 3. https://www.wsj.com/articles/iran-u-s-press-ahead-with-efforts-to-seal-nuclear-deal-by-month-end-1425393719.

Nye, Joseph S. 1990. *Bound to Lead: The Changing Nature of American Power*. New York: Basic Books.

———. 2004. *Soft Power: The Means to Success in World Politics*. New York: Public Affairs.

Obama, Michelle. 2018. *Becoming*. London: Viking.

Oh, Kwang-Jin. 2018. "Chungguk "Kimjŏngŭn 19–20il Pangjung" Ch'Ŏt Sajŏnbodo . . . Chŏngsanggukka Imiji Noryŏ." *Chosun*, June 19. http://news.chosun.com/site/data/html_dir/2018/06/19/2018061901606.html.

Orbán, Viktor. 2021a. "Magyar ember három esetben térdel le: Isten, a haza és a szerelme előtt." *Facebook*, June 10. https://www.facebook.com/watch/?v=514938296488325.

Orbán, Viktor. 2021b. "A cserkész, ahol tud, segít." *Facebook*, August 28. https://www.facebook.com/photo/?fbid=384010296429908&set=a.347694613394810.

Orbán, Viktor. 2021c. "Element a Profi." *Facebook*, September 6. https://www.facebook.com/orbanviktor/posts/390225462475058.

Papacharissi, Zizi. 2015. *Affective Publics: Sentiment, Technology, and Politics*. New York: Oxford University Press.

———. 2019. "Forget Messiahs." *Social Media and Society* 5, no. 3:205630511984971.

———. 2021. *After Democracy: Imagining Our Political Future*. New Haven. CT: Yale University Press.

Park, Kyung-Man. 2018. "Chŏngbu Chaje Yoch'Ŏngedo . . . T'Albukchadanch'E 'Sil P'Ajusŏ Taebukchŏndan Salp'O.'" *Hankyoreh*, May 4. http://www.hani.co.kr/arti/society/area/843336.html.

Park, Soo-Hyun. 2018. "Risŏlchu Tonghaengdo P'Agyŏk . . . P'Ŏsŭt'Ŭreidiro Kukche Oegyo Tebwi." *Chosun*, March 28. http://news.chosun.com/site/data /html_dir/2018/03/28/2018032802194.html.

Park, Sun-Ha. 2018. "'P'Yŏngyangnaengmyŏn Patko Yangnyŏmch'Ik'in Chuja': Chŏlmŭn'Gŏttŭrŭi Pallarhan P'Yŏnghwa Kŭrigi." *Hankyoreh*, May 17. http:// www.hani.co.kr/arti/economy/economy_general/845092.html.

Parker, Ashley, and Anna Fifield. 2018. "Pence's Olympic Mission: Countering North Korean Propaganda." *Washingtonpost.com*, February 9. https://www .washingtonpost.com/politics/pences-olympic-mission--rebuff-north-koreas -propaganda/2018/02/09/6140f7b4-0d9c-11e8-baf5-e629fc1cd21e_story.html.

Perlez, Jane. 2018. "Kim Jong-un's China Visit Strengthens His Hand in Nuclear Talks." *International New York Times*, March 28. https://www.nytimes.com /2018/03/28/world/asia/china-kim-north-korea-visit.html.

Peters, John Durham. 1993. "Distrust of Representation: Habermas on the Public Sphere." *Media, Culture and Society* 15, no. 4:541–71.

Place, Nathan. 2021. 'I Don't Want to Rattle the Kids': The Moment George W. Bush Learned 9/11 Had Happened." *Independent*, September 1. https://www .the-independent.com/news/world/americas/us-politics/9-11-george-bush -reaction-school-b1902343.html.

Poulakidakos, Stamatis, and Iliana Giannouli. 2019. "Greek Political Leaders on Instagram: Between "Soft" and "Hard" Personalization." In *Visual Political Communication*, edited by Anastasia Veneti, Daniel Jackson, and Darren G. Lilleker, 187–206. Cham: Springer.

Pressler, Jessica. 2017. "This Stanford Professor Has a Theory on Why 2017 Is Filled with Jerks." *New York Magazine*, September 20. https://nymag.com /intelligencer/2017/09/robert-sutton-asshole-survival-guide.html.

Rai, Swapnil. 2019. "'May the Force Be with You': Narendra Modi and the Celebritization of Indian Politics." *Communication, Culture and Critique* 12, no. 3:323–39.

Ravid, Barak. 2015. "Zarif: Iran Saved Jews Three Times—Netanyahu Should Learn History." *Haaretz*, March 5. https://www.haaretz.co.il/news/politics /1.2581775/.

Rényi, Pál Dániel. 2021. *Győzelmi kényszer: Futball és hatalom Orbán világában.* Budapest: Magyar Jeti.

Rényi, Pál Dániel, and Mark Herczeg. 2022. "Legyőzhetetlen Orbán Viktor pártállami kampánygépezete." *444.hu*, April 25. https://444.hu/tldr/2022/04/25 /legyozhetetlen-orban-viktor-partallami-kampanygepezete.

Repnikova, Maria. 2018. *Media Politics in China: Improvising Power under Authoritarianism.* Cambridge: Cambridge University Press.

Reuters. 2015. "Iran's Foreign Minister Summoned over Walk with Kerry." *Reuters*, January 25. https://www.reuters.com/article/us-iran-nuclear-usa /irans-foreign-minister-summoned-to-parliament-over-walk-with-kerry -idUSKBN0KY0MB20150125.

Rich, Motoko. 2018. "Unscripted Moments Steal the Show at Trump-Kim Singapore Summit." *International New York Times*, June 13. https://www.nytimes.com/2018/06/12/world/asia/trump-kim-summit-theatrics.html.

Rich, Motoko, and Choe Sang-Hun. 2018. "Kim Jong-un's Sister Turns on the Charm, Taking Pence's Spotlight." *New York Times* (online), February 11. https://www.nytimes.com/2018/02/11/world/asia/kim-yo-jong-mike-pence-olympics.html.

Sajó, András, Renáta Uitz, and Stephen T. Holmes. 2022. *Routledge Handbook of Illiberalism*. London: Routledge, Taylor and Francis.

Sandberg, Sheryl. 2018. "Jacinda Ardern." *Time*. https://time.com/collection/most-influential-people-2018/5217549/jacinda-ardern-2/.

Sanger, David. 2015. "No. 2 Negotiators in Iran Talks Argue Physics behind Politics." *New York Times*, March 29. https://www.nytimes.com/2015/03/29/world/middleeast/no-2-negotiators-in-iran-talks-argue-physics-behind-politics.html.

Sauder, Michael. 2020. "A Sociology of Luck." *Sociological Theory* 38, no. 3:193–216.

Sauerbrey, Anna. 2021. "Farewell, Angela Merkel. You Were Once the 'Leader of the Free World.'" *New York Times*, September 24. https://www.nytimes.com/2021/09/24/opinion/angela-merkel-germany-election.html.

Scannell, Paddy. 2014. *Television and the Meaning of 'Live': An Enquiry into the Human Situation*. New York: Polity.

Schneider, Y. 2013. "The Master of Smiles: Who Are You Muhammad Zarif?" *Mako*, November 30. https://www.mako.co.il/news-world/international/Article-fa5628abb4aa241004.htm.

Sheafer, Tamir. 2001. "Charismatic Skill and Media Legitimacy: An Actor-Centered Approach to Understanding the Political Communication Competition." Communication Research 28, no. 6:711–36.

Shils, Edward. 1965. "Charisma, Order, and Status." *American Sociological Review* 30, no. 2:199–213.

Shivaram, Deepa, and Avie Schneider. 2022. "Biden Says of Putin: 'For God's Sake, This Man Cannot Remain in Power.'" *NPR*, March 26. https://www.npr.org/2022/03/26/1089014039/biden-says-of-putin-for-gods-sake-this-man-cannot-remain-in-power.

Silverman, Mike. 2023. "Don Giovanni Is "Unredeemable" in Ivo Van Hove's US Opera Debut." *AP News*, May 3. https://apnews.com/article/don-giovanni-met-ivo-van-hove-9c5477ddc3a312aa4253919044bbd65b.

Solomon, Jay. 2015a. "GOP Letter Emerges as Issue in Iran Talks; Letter by Republicans That Raises Doubts about a Deal Wasn't 'Helpful' to the Negotiations, Official Says." *Wall Street Journal: Eastern Edition*, March 16. https://www.wsj.com/articles/u-k-s-hammond-says-iran-nuclear-deal-closer-but-still-long-way-to-go-1426519427.

———. 2015b. "In Iran Nuclear Talks, Two MIT-Connected Physicists Play Key Roles; U.S. Energy Secretary, Iranian Atomic Agency Chairman Hash Out

Details amid the Diplomacy." *Wall Street Journal: Eastern Edition*, March 17. https://www.wsj.com/articles/in-iran-nuclear-talks-two-mit-trained-physicists -play-key-roles-1426624253.

Solomon, Jay, and Laurence Norman. 2015a. "France Takes Toughest Line at Iran Nuclear Talks; Negotiations Move Closer to March 31 Cutoff without a Breakthrough." *Wall Street Journal: Eastern Edition*, March 20. https://www.wsj.com /articles/european-leaders-discuss-iran-nuclear-talks-1426845251.

———. 2015b. "Iran Stalls U.N. Probe into Its Atomic Past; Talks over Iran's Nuclear Program Have Hit a Stumbling Block Because Tehran Has Failed to Cooperate with a United Nations Probe into Whether It Tried to Build Atomic Weapons in the Past." *Wall Street Journal: Eastern Edition*, March 25. https:// www.wsj.com/articles/iran-stalls-u-n-probe-into-its-1427327943.

Sonnevend, Julia. 2016. *Stories Without Borders: The Berlin Wall and the Making of a Global Iconic Event*. New York: Oxford University Press.

———. 2018. "Facts (Almost) Never Win over Myths." In *Trump and the Media*, edited by Pablo J. Boczkowski and Zizi Papacharissi, 87–92. Boston: MIT Press.

———. 2019. "Charm Offensive: Mediatized Country Image Transformations in International Relations." *Information, Communication and Society* 22, no. 5:695–701.

———. 2024. "Populist Iconicity: The Contradictions of Hungarian Prime Minister Viktor Orbán as a Political Celebrity." *Journal of Media and Cinema Studies* 63, no. 2:169–75.

Sonnevend, Julia, and Yuval Katz. 2020. "Capturing Hearts: The Coverage of Iran's Charm Offensive during the 2015 Nuclear Deal Negotiations in the American and Israeli Press." *Journalism Studies* 21, no. 11:1551–70.

Sonnevend, Julia, and Youngrim Kim. 2020. "An Unlikely Seducer: Kim Jong-un's Charm Offensive from the PyeongChang Winter Olympics until the Trump-Kim Summit." *International Journal of Communication* 14:1398–420.

Sonnevend, Julia, and Veronika Kövesdi. 2023. "More Than Just a Strongman: The Strategic Construction of Viktor Orbán's Charismatic Authority on Facebook." *International Journal of Press/Politics*, first published online June 14. https:// journals.sagepub.com/doi/10.1177/19401612231179120.

Sonnevend, Julia, and Olivia Steiert. 2022. "The Power of Predictability: How Angela Merkel Constructed Her Authenticity on Instagram." *New Media and Society*, first published online December 8. https://doi.org/10.1177/14614448221138472.

Sorensen, Lone. 2021. *Populist Communication: Ideology, Performance, Mediation*. Cham, Switzerland: Palgrave Macmillan.

Steffan, Dennis. 2020. "Visual Self-Presentation Strategies of Political Candidates on Social Media Platforms: A Comparative Study." *International Journal of Communication* 14:3096–118.

Suh, J.-Y, and G.-J Yoo. 1997. "Kimilsŏng Ihu Puk'Anŭi Taeoe Chŏngch'Aek: Ch'Ogukkajŏk Kwan'Gye, Kungnae Chŏngch'i Kujo, Taeoe Chŏngch'Aek Pyŏnhwaŭi Tonghak." *Asea Yŏn'Gu* 40, no. 1:43–67.

Sutton, Robert I. 2007. *The No Asshole Rule*: Concentrated Knowledge for the Busy Executive. Boston: Grand Central.

———. 2010. *Good Boss, Bad Boss: How to Be the Best and Learn from the Worst.* Concentrated Knowledge for the Busy Executive. New York: Business Plus.

———. 2017. *The Asshole Survival Guide*. Boston: HarperCollins.

Szabó, András. 2022. "Inside Orbán's Fidesz Party Preparing for Hungary's Parliamentary Election." *Direkt36.Hu*, March 11. https://www.direkt36.hu/en/orban-asztalan-sorakozo-szines-cetlik-mutatjak-hogyan-ujitotta-meg-a-kampanyat-a-fidesz/.

Szebeni, Zea, and Virpi Salojärvi. 2022. "'Authentically' Maintaining Populism in Hungary—Visual Analysis of Prime Minister Viktor Orbán's Instagram." *Mass Communication and Society* 25, no. 6:812–37.

Szelényi, Zsuzsanna. 2023. *Tainted Democracy: Viktor Orbán and the Subversion of Hungary*. La Vergne: Hurst.

Taub, Amanda. 2023. "Jacinda Ardern Says No to Burnout." *New York Times*, January 20. https://www.nytimes.com/2023/01/20/world/asia/jacinda-ardern-burnout.html.

Tharoor, Ishan. 2018. "What Did Pence Achieve at the Olympics?" *The Washington Post*, February 13. https://www.washingtonpost.com/news/worldviews/wp/2018/02/13/what-did-pence-achieve-at-the-olympics/.

The Times. 2011. "Profile of Viktor Orbán: A Charismatic and Ruthless Political Operator." *The Times*, January 1. https://www.thetimes.co.uk/article/profile-of-viktor-orban-a-charismatic-and-ruthless-political-operator-ljdwbg8gkq8.

Tracy, Brian, and Ron Arden. 2006. *The Power of Charm: How to Win Anyone Over in Any Situation*. New York: Amacom.

Trump, Mary L. 2020. *Too Much and Never Enough: How My Family Created the World's Most Dangerous Man*. Hardback ed. London: Simon and Schuster.

Tworek, Heidi, Ian Beacock, and Eseohe Ojo. 2020. "Democratic Health Communications during Covid-19: A RAPID Response." September. https://democracy2017.sites.olt.ubc.ca/files/2020/09/Democratic-Health-Communication-during-Covid_FINAL.pdf.

Van Aelst, Peter, Tamir Sheafer, and James Stanyer. 2012. "The Personalization of Mediated Political Communication: A Review of Concepts, Operationalizations and Key Findings." *Journalism Studies* 13, no. 2:203–20.

Wagner-Pacifici, Robin. 2017. *What Is an Event?* Chicago: University of Chicago Press.

———. 2023. "Anticharismatic Authority: Joe Biden's Approximation of the Ideal Type." *Politics and Society*, first published online March 22. https://journals.sagepub.com/doi/full/10.1177/00323292231158915.

Walker, Shaun. 2018. "'You Cannot Negotiate with Orbán': Hardline PM Seeks Fourth Term." *Guardian* (London), April 6. https://www.theguardian.com/world/2018/apr/06/hungary-viktor-orban-election-migration.

Wall Street Journal Editorial Board. 2018. "The Pyongyang Olympics: The Western Media Discover the Hidden Charms of North Korea." *Wall Street Journal*

Eastern Edition, February 11. https://www.wsj.com/articles/the-pyongyang
-olympics-1518383959.

Washington Post Staff. 2015. "The Complete Transcript of Netanyahu's Address to
Congress." *Washington Post*, March 3. https://www.washingtonpost.com/news
/post-politics/wp/2015/03/03/full-text-netanyahus-address-to-congress/.

Weber, Max. 1947. *The Theory of Social and Economic Organization*. Edited by Talc-
ott Parsons. New York: Free Press.

———. 1968. *Economy and Society*. German original published in 1922. Edited by
Guenther Roth and Claus Wittich. Los Angeles: University of California Press.

Women in the World. 2019. "Oprah Winfrey's Leadership Advice: 'Channel Your
Own Inner Jacindas.'" Women of the World Summit, New York. https://www
.youtube.com/watch?v=w89tivkd0bk&t=1s.

Wright, Robin. 2015. "A New Year in Iran?" *New Yorker*, March 20. https://www
.newyorker.com/news/news-desk/a-new-year-in-iran.

Yang, Sung-Un, Hochang Shin, Jong-Hyuk Lee, and Brenda Wrigley. 2008. "Country Reputation in Multidimensions: Predictors, Effects, and Communication
Channels." *Journal of Public Relations Research* 20, no. 4:421–40.

Yoo, Yu-Won. 2018. "Mi, Chŏllyangmugi Chŏnjinbaech'I . . . Puk Haesangch'Adan
K'Adŭdo Kkŏnaetta." *Chosun*, January 18. http://news.chosun.com/site/data
/html_dir/2018/01/18/2018011800129.html.

Yoon, H.-S. 2018. "Pukkwaŭi Kyŏngje Hyŏmnyŏk, Kach'Iwa Mokp'Yo Soge
Ch'Ujindwaeya Handa." *Chosun*, May 14. http://news.chosun.com/site/data
/html_dir/2018/05/13/2018051301797.html.

Young, Jeremy C. 2016. *The Age of Charisma: Leaders, Followers, and Emotions in
American Society, 1879–1940*. Cambridge: Cambridge University Press.

Zarif, Mohammad Javad. 2014. "What Iran Really Wants: Iranian Foreign Policy in
the Rouhani Era." *Foreign Affairs*, May 1, 49–59.

ZDF Politbarometer. n.d. "Wie Macht Angela Merkel Ihre Arbeit Als Bundeskanzlerin Alles in Allem Gesehen?" https://de.statista.com/statistik/daten
/studie/675140/umfrage/bewertung-der-arbeit-von-angela-merkel-als
-bundeskanzlerin/. Accessed January 20, 2024.

Zhang, Juyan, and William L. Benoit. 2004. "Message Strategies of Saudi Arabia's Image Restoration Campaign after 9 / 11." *Public Relations Review* 30,
no. 2:161–67.

INDEX

Page numbers in *italics* refer to illustrations.